Voicing New Questions for

Eleasah P. Louis and Andy Goodliff
(editors)

Voicing New Questions for Baptist Identity

Eleasah P. Louis and Andy Goodliff
(editors)

Regent's Park College, Oxford

Regent's Park College is a Permanent Private Hall of the University of Oxford.

Centre for Baptist Studies in Oxford
(formerly the Centre for Baptist History and Heritage)
Regent's Park College, Pusey Street, Oxford OX1 2LB
(Regent's Park College is a Permanent Private Hall
of the University of Oxford)
www.rpc.ox.ac.uk

19 18 17 16 15 14 13   7 6 5 4 3 2 1

British Library Cataloguing in Publication Data
A catalogue record for this book is available from the British

Library ISBN 9798867019426

Cover Illustrations: Laura James, Fish for Breakfast, 2000
Used with permission.

Copy-edited by the editors

Table of Contents

Contributors

Pam Davies is minister of Southend City Baptist Church, Southend-on-Sea.

Andy Goodliff is minister of Belle Vue Baptist Church, Southend-on-Sea and Lecturer in Baptist History, Regent's Park College, Oxford.

Leigh Greenwood is minister of Stoneygate Baptist Church, Leicester.

Martin Hobgen is minister of Swaythling Baptist Church, Southampton.

Simon Jay is Community Development Worker at the Haven Community Project, Birmingham.

Tim Judson is Lecturer in Ministerial Formation, Regent's Park College, Oxford.

Eleasah P. Louis is a Research and Resource Developer who has worked for the Baptist Union of Great Britain.

Ruth Moriarty is minister of Christ Church New Southgate/Friern Barnet (Baptist/URC).

Anthony Reddie is Professor of Black Theology, University of Oxford and Director of the Centre for Religion and Culture, Regent's Park College, Oxford.

Tomos Roberts-Young is minister of Noddfa Newydd Baptist Chapel, Neath, Wales.

Preface

In 1986, Brian Haymes, who had recently been appointed Principal of Northern Baptist College, gave a set of addresses to the Yorkshire Baptist Association. Afterwards, they were published by the Association under the title *A Question of Identity: Reflections on Baptist Principles and Practice*.[1] Haymes wanted to remind people of the key aspects of 'our' Baptist identity — ecclesial, political, and confessional — that he felt were in danger of being disregarded or abused. Twenty-five years later, Haymes was given a festschrift with the title *Questions of Identity*,[2] which acknowledged the influence of the earlier little booklet and offered some more engagements with Baptist identity. The title of the present book echoes in part Haymes' title — Baptist identity is its focus — at the same time, it wants to introduce new questions to the task of Baptist identity from the perspectives of race, gender, disability, nationality, and sexuality.

The origin of this book was a recognition that most Baptist theological reflection has been done by white, male scholars.[3]

---

[1] The lectures were republished in 2021 in *Journal of Baptist Theology in Context*, issue 4, with Haymes adding a new coda.

[2] Anthony R. Cross and Ruth Gouldbourne (eds.), *Questions of Identity: Studies in Honour of Brian Haymes* (Oxford: Regent's Park College, 2011).

[3] We might note, for example, the names of Paul S. Fiddes, *Tracks and Traces* (Carlisle: Paternoster, 2003), Nigel Wright, *Free Church, Free State* (Milton Keynes: Paternoster, 2005), Brian Haymes, *A Question of Identity* (Yorkshire Baptist Association, 1986), John E. Colwell, *Promise and Presence*

While their work has been and is valuable — making important contributions to the thinking and practices of Baptist life and worship — it has not generally been attentive to the voices of black, female, disabled, non-English, and LGBT Baptist lives. It is the intention of *Voicing New Questions for Baptist Identity* to seek to make a modest contribution to opening the Baptist conversation to the more diverse context we now inhabit.[4]

In the introductory chapter to his important book *Tracks and Traces*, Paul Fiddes has argued that a Baptist way of doing theology will attend to the experience, the confession, and the stories, of a community.[5] The chapters that follow will introduce experiences and stories from Baptist communities that have been absent or overlooked from the task of identifying and articulating who we are as a Baptist people. This has implications for our confession of faith. Baptist identity is not something static but is always an on-going conversation between the past and the present.

(Milton Keynes: Paternoster, 2005), Paul Beasley-Murray, *Radical Believers* (2nd Ed.; Didcot: Baptist Union, 2006), Christopher J. Ellis, *Gathering: A Theology and Spirituality of Worship in Free Church Tradition* (London: SCM, 2004), and Stephen R. Holmes, *Baptist Theology* (London: T & T Clark, 2012).

[4] Elsewhere I have highlighted the story what might be called a 'summons to be heard' by women and black voices, see Andy Goodliff, 'A Summons to be Heard: Towards a More Just Baptist Identity', *Journal for European Baptist Studies* 22.1 (2022): 21-36.

[5] Fiddes, *Tracks and Traces*, 3-12.

Ruth Moriarty draws on her doctoral research into the practice of the church meeting, highlighting the uncomfortable fact that racism can be and is often, consciously, or not, in play when Baptists seek to discern the mind of Christ. Simon Jay explores how our celebration of the Lord's Supper might develop if we attend to other cultural traditions. Leigh Greenwood reflects on being a Baptist minister and a mother of two children, engaging with how these two vocations interact with each other. Martin Hobgen argues that more attention need to be given to how persons with disability are viewed and included in church life. Pam Davies considers conversations she hosted between Baptist ministers and LGBT Baptist church members on how Baptists might find ways to better talk together about sexuality. Tomos Roberts-Young studies the impact of contemporary worship songs on the Welsh practice of singing. Eleasah P. Louis asks whether the Baptist tradition of dissent might learn something from the stories and experiences of the young Black exodus from the church. Finally, Tim Judson, reflecting from the experience of a partial loss of eyesight, argues that we should take far more seriously the importance of particularity and context for our being church and disciples.

The book ends with an afterword from Anthony Reddie. Reddie's own church story is a long association with the Methodists, but he has been and continues to be a friend to Baptists,[6] and offers his reflections on the essays in that spirit.

---

[6] Since 2020 he has been Director of the Centre for Religion and Culture at Regent's Park College, where many of his colleagues are Baptists. He also

The impact of this book will not only be in how the chapters within are received, but whether it continues a questioning and exploring Baptist identity that is attentive to all the voices within its gatherings, whether they be local, regional, or national.

Andy Goodliff
All Saints' Day, 2023

---

worked for a year at Bristol Baptist College. He collaborated with other Baptists in 2017 on *Journeying to Justice: Contributions to the Baptist tradition across the Black Atlantic* (Milton Keynes: Paternoster, 2017).

1 Racism and the Church Meeting

Ruth Moriarty

The Baptist Church Meeting is a key component of Baptist church life as it provides a distinctive theological pattern for discernment: slow wisdom.[7] Participating in discerning the mind of Christ is challenging however for those who are different to the majority of church members. Younger members, members from another denomination and Black[8] and Brown church members are less likely to be heard and agreed with at the Church Meeting. If the Church Meeting does not listen to all members, it limits discernment to the opinion of the historic norm of the church.

It is a core Baptist belief that every member of the church is part of the priesthood of all believers through whom the Spirit speaks (1 Peter 2.4-5). At the Church Meeting members are invited to discern the mind of Christ together, and yet the typical experience

---

[7] For a more extensive account of slow wisdom see Ruth Moriarty, *How do Baptists Discern the Mind of Christ at the Church Meeting?* (University of Chester, DProf, 2023).

[8] I have capitalised Black, Brown and White in order to engage with a form of orthographic justice which 'consciously chooses to capitalize Black, Brown, Indigenous, and White, we can take a small step towards a more just and inclusive world.' John Palfrey and Kristen Mack, MacArthur Foundation, Capitalizing Black and White: Grammatical Justice and Equity, Accessed online: https://www.macfound.org/press/perspectives/capitalizing-Black-and-White-grammatical-justice-and-equity (May, 2020).

of a Church Meeting is one of inertia, conflict and low attendance. This paper is part of a larger project that sought to understand how Baptists discern together at the Church Meeting. Qualitative research methods were used to analyse data about discernment processes by observing four London Baptist churches and interviewing the minister and two church members from each participant church. The project shows that church members who are different to the majority of members find it difficult to participate in discernment. In particular, members who are younger or from another denomination often fail to attend or engage with the Church Meeting. Furthermore, the project data shows that while Black and Brown church members are present, their views are less likely to be heard and agreed with at the Church Meeting. This is problematic to Baptists as it contradicts our belief that the Spirit may speak through any church member.

Overall, my hope is to foster confidence for Baptists in discernment at the Church Meeting. The project identifies the Baptist discernment process as *slow wisdom*, which is a positive and distinctive element of Baptist church practice. Slow wisdom rests on the principles of slowness, prayer and listening to others. If the Church Meeting does not listen to Black and Brown members, the slow wisdom of discernment is harder to discover. To analyse the data, an intersectional approach is taken to explore themes of relationality, social context and racism at the Church Meeting. This analysis enables a deeper recognition of layers of power at work as identified by Patricia Collins and Sirma Bilge.[9]

---

[9] Patricia Hill Collins and Sirma Bilge, *Intersectionality* (Cambridge:

Willie Jennings shows how the affection and design of theological education limits the participation of Black and Brown students at university.[10] Jennings' analysis provides a pattern for understanding racism at the Church Meeting. This chapter proposes the practical suggestion of group work to begin to address racism at the Church Meeting in order that all members may participate in discernment at the Church Meeting.

Analysing the Church Meeting: An Intersectional Approach

The intersectional approach[11] as proposed by Collins and Blige suggests:

> a way of understanding and analysing the complexity in the world, in people, and in human experiences. The events and conditions of social and political life and the self can seldom be understood as shaped by one factor. They are generally shaped by many factors in diverse and mutually influencing ways.[12]

Polity, 2016).

[10] Willie James Jennings. *After Whiteness: An education in belonging* (Grand Rapids, MI: Eerdmans, 2020).

[11] Collins and Bilge follow Kimberle Crenshaw's original intersectional analysis approach in 'Mapping the Margins: Intersectionality, Identity Politics, and Violence against Women of Color,' *Stanford Law Review* 43.6 (July 1991): 1241-1299.

[12] Collins and Bilge, *Intersectionality*, 2.

Collins and Bilge's model of analysis considers six core ideas: multi-inequalities, relationality, power, social context, complexity, and social justice.[13] For the purposes of this short chapter, analysis is centred on three areas: the relationality of myself as a White researcher and the project participants, the social context of the participant churches, and racism at Church Meetings by using axial coding[14] on the project data. This intersectional approach offers a contextual reflection that recognises the complexity of the Church Meeting and seeks to make helpful change to practice.

Relationality as a Researcher

Early in the interview stage of the project I met Desmond[15] the first Black minister of Hedger[16] Baptist Church who opened the

---

[13] Collins and Bilge, *Intersectionality*, 25-26.

[14] For a description of axial coding methodology and its uses see K. Charmaz, *Constructing Grounded Theory*. 2nd ed. (London: SAGE, 2014).

[15] All participants' names have been anonymised.

[16] 2019 was the centenary for the ordination of women in the Baptist Church. In tribute, the names of four historical women ministers were used to anonymously refer to participant churches. Edith Gates had a flourishing ministry in 1918 at Cleveley, Violet Hedger was the first woman to be trained for ministry at Regent's Park College Oxford in 1919, Margaret Jarman was the first female President of the Baptist Union 1987 and Kate Coleman was the first Black woman to become an accredited Baptist minister in 1996 and President of the Baptist Union in 2006. Gates, Hedger, Jarman and Coleman are the references for the four churches that participated in this project. Baptist Union Project Violet (2019), [accessed online at: https://www.baptist.org.uk/Groups/363245/Project_Violet.aspx].

question of relationality and research for me. He recounted a conversation he had with the previous treasurer at his church as follows:

> Desmond: He was concerned that church was becoming too Black.
> Ruth: Was he White?
> Desmond: Yeah.

Hearing Desmond's experience of racism was a poignant moment in fieldwork for me. As a researcher informed by fifteen years of ministerial practice, I had expected to observe and discover plenty of stories around power, silencing of women and low attendance at Church Meetings in comparison to Sunday worship services. Such expectations were formed by the experience of attending four different Baptist churches as a White female middle-class member or as a minister. However, these expectations were challenged by listening to Desmond's early experience as a Black minister in an historically White Baptist church.

On reflection, I realised that Desmond's story required a new kind of listening, in which it would be important to acknowledge my position and biases. I explore my privilege of Whiteness as a minister and researcher below. Both Desmond and I shared a commonality: being a Baptist minister in London. Vron Ware and Les Back argue relationality between the participant and the researcher helps to 'avoid the construction of simplified and hermetic distinctions between empirical objects of research and the recondite position of the ethnographer.'[17]   Our shared relationality as ministers meant that I was able to offer a 'cousin' position as a researcher whereby both interviewer and interviewee speak the same language, understand nuances and recognise family problems.[18] As a White woman, I could not appreciate Desmond's pain of experiencing racism, but I felt grateful to those participating in the project who graciously shared their stories of exclusion.

In order to understand Desmond's experience of racism, I explored my privilege of Whiteness. Robert Beckford states: 'Whiteness is more than just the epidermis, it is also about behavioural characteristics, social location and world-view'.[19] My world view as a White researcher was typified by Lorraine Dixon's observation that: 'Good White Christian folks often cannot believe how racism and other forms of oppression can limit the experience of many within the church'.[20] Being White in an historically White church means that I can view all church

---

[17] Vron Ware and Les Back, *Out of whiteness: Colour, Politics and Culture* (Chicago: University of Chicago, 2002), 40.
[18] See O. Karnieli-Miller, R. Strier and L Pesach, 'Power relations in Qualitative Research', *Qualitative Health Research*, 19.2 (2009): 279-89.
[19] Robert Beckford, 'Dread and Rahtid: Robert Beckford's Canon' in *Black Theology in Britain: A Reader* edited by Michael Jagessar and Anthony Reddie (London: Routledge, 2007), 100.
[20] Lorraine Dixon, 'bell hooks: Teller of Truth and Dreamer of Dreams' in *Black Theology in Britain: A Reader* edited by Michael Jagessar and Anthony Reddie (London: Routledge, 2007), 126.

practices, habits and beliefs held by my church as normal. Beginning with participation in worship, Tope Bello argues that: 'to look like an authentic Christian you must sing, worship, and act in a way that is Western'.[21] Kate Coleman, who was the first Black female minister to be President of the Union, states that throughout her training for ministry 'the only valid theology presented was patriarchal and invariably Euro-American'.[22] Furthermore, Baptist minister Michelle Mahon writes regarding the need for wholesale structural change in Baptist churches:

There is a necessity for abandonment of the notion that 'Whiteness' is normative and central to Christian reality, yet this process of abandonment is not a simple task because the organisational structures within the world's major churches are inextricably bound up with Whiteness.[23]

In sum, Whiteness is the norm in Baptist Union churches in the UK. As Bello, Coleman and Mahon suggest Whiteness is seen in the practice of worship, in ministerial training and organisational

---

[21] Tope Bello, 'Reflections of a Second-Generation African Christian in Britain' in *World Christianity in Western Europe: Diasporic Identity, Narratives & Missiology* edited by Israel Oluwole Olofinjana (Oxford: Regnum, 2020), 46.

[22] Kate Coleman, 'Black Theology and Black Liberation: a Womanist Perspective' in *Black Theology in Britain: A Reader* edited by Michael Jagessar and Anthony Reddie (London: Routledge, 2007), 112.

[23] Michelle Mahon, 'Sisters with voices': a study of the experiences and challenges face by black women in London Baptist Association church ministry settings', *Black Theology* 13.3 (2015): 288.

structure. Ware and Back state that an acknowledgment of Whiteness 'must be coupled with a commitment to achieving social justice through understanding how racism functions and therefore how it can be dismantled.'[24] The observation of this project is that Whiteness is present within White researchers like myself and within the observed Church Meetings in this project.

Social Context: Demographic Changes in London

Local demographic changes have important effects on the social context and experience of racism at the Church Meeting. The multi-layered nature of intersectional analysis fosters a broader framework to explore the original conversation with Desmond about the ex-treasurer at Hedger. Desmond continued recounting his narrative of the encounter:

> Desmond: He was concerned that church was becoming too Black.
> Ruth: Was he White?
> Desmond: Yeah.
> Desmond: I thought 'oh where has this come from?' And I think it came out wrong.
> Ruth: That's always gonna come out wrong! I mean there is no right way to say that, oh gosh!
> Desmond: I think what he wanted to say, was that what he had noticed was that the White folks were either dying out or passing on or moving on to better areas outside the

---

[24] Ware and Back, *Out of Whiteness*, 58.

M25. And that the people coming in were more mixed. I think that's what he meant. I said to him: 'Look I have no control over who comes, or what colour they are.'

Desmond outlines a changing social context for Hedger Baptist, which was typical of each church in this project. All sample churches were White historically but had changed to become multi-ethnic congregations. The mix of ethnicities of each of the sample churches has changed in each of the participants' recent memory. This directly reflects the consistently changing demographic of people living and working in London. Linbert Spencer identifies that 'London's ethnic make-up is constantly evolving. For centuries, the city has been the first destination for most people migrating to Britain.'[25] For example, in my London borough[26] where the majority of the sample churches are located a noticeable decrease in the White population was identified in the 2011 census: The White UK ethnic group is 40.5% which is a sharp fall from the 2001 level (for White British) of 61.2%. The White UK share is lower than in both London as a whole (44.9%) and well below the level in England (79.8%) (My London Council, 2012).[27]

---

[25] Linbert Spencer, *Building a Multi-ethnic Church* (London: SPCK, 2007), 56.

[26] My London Council denotes the location of the research project and so is anonymised.

[27] *My London Council, Communities, Communications, Policy and Performance: Briefing note on 2011 Census – Ethnicity, Country of Birth, Faith and Main Language, Accessed: https://new.gov.uk/services/your-council/census-and-socio-economic-information/about-information-2011-

At Hedger Baptist, the church became a Black majority church in an historically White denomination. Anthony Reddie states, there are two types of Black churches, namely Pentecostal or Black majority, and that: 'these churches are demographically determined, as their Black majority membership has grown out of Black migrants moving into inner-city urban contexts, coupled with the flight of the White middle class.'[28] Desmond suggests further explanations for a shifting demographic context: new stages in life and economic rationale. Likewise, Omar Khan identifies the effects of parenthood and gentrification as part of the reason for demographic change in London and other large cities.[29] Change within the social context of Hedger Baptist for reasons of white flight, economic pressure and change within individual families contributed to Desmond's experience of racism within his church.

Axial Coding: Speech, Power and Racism

This qualitative research project gathers data from participants in Baptist churches through observation and interviews. Interviews were coded thematically to gather data into categories such as

---

census-ethnicity-language-faith-country-of-origin.pdf, [30/9/19]

[28] Anthony Reddie, 'Black Theology in Britain' in *The Cambridge Companion to Black Theology* edited by Dwight Hopkins and Edward P. Antonio (Cambridge: Cambridge University Press, 2012), 237.

[29] Omar Khan (2019). '*False fears of 'white flight' in London and elsewhere*' https://www.runnymedetrust.org/blog/false-fears-of-white-flight-in-london-and-elsewhere Accessed: 12/7/21.

conflict, prayer, racism. A second cycle of axial coding was completed to further analyse each thematic category. Axial coding was selected for this purpose as it encourages the researcher to identify the contexts, conditions, interactions and consequences'[30] within each thematic category. Strauss and Corbin[31] created axial coding as a method to 'produce categories that perform two functions: they have to express what the theory is about and they have to express how they relate to each other.'[32] However, Charmaz argues axial coding is an unhelpful method as strategies ought to be 'emergent from data'[33] and not be applied to data. For the purposes of this project, axial coding is used because it provides a visible framework to ask the same questions of each category. Moreover, in order to answer the research topic; how Baptists discern the mind of Christ, identifying the relationship between categories shows an outline argument from the data. To mitigate Charmaz's concern, I adopt Cory Labanow's method on researching the local church by providing coding method information and a 'thick' description of the data.[34] The following example from Desmond of how this approach operates

[30] Johnny Saldana, *The Coding Manual for Qualitative Researchers*. 3rd Edition (London: SAGE, 2016), 244.

[31] Anselm Strauss and Juliet Corbin, *Basics of qualitative research: Grounded theory procedures and techniques* (UK: SAGE, 1990).

[32] Barry Gibson and Jan Hartman, *Rediscovering Grounded Theory* (London: SAGE, 2014), 98.

[33] Kathy Charmaz, *Constructing Grounded Theory*. 2nd Edition. (London: SAGE, 2014), 144.

[34] Cory Labanow in *Practical Theology and Qualitative Research* edited by John Swinton and Harriet Mowat (London: SCM Press, 2006), 149.

is seen in the presentation of a 'thick' description and then axial coding analysis below.

Jamaican born, Black minister Desmond shared what he considered a challenge to discernment where different terms of expression are used by Black Nigerian and White British members at the Church Meeting:

> Desmond: It's partly cultural, both in their different ways [*two Black Nigerian members*] are very forward and clear in the way they would express things. Maybe [*the White British secretary*] and I would be more diplomatic. We'd probably say the same thing but in a more diplomatic way and certainly I think [*the White British secretary*] feel that there are certain things that are best not said. Whereas [*two Black Nigerian members*] would …
>
> Ruth: Just say it! [both laugh]

Axial coding asks the researcher to consider what is the condition, context, action, consequence of each code and if it links to other parts of the project data.

Sample axial coding

Desmond (Transcript page 14, code 27)	
Condition	Overall theme of difficultly in discernment.

Context	Different terms of expression used by Black and White members.
Action	The non-verbal result was a source of tension within the Meeting.
Consequence	'Puts people off coming'
Linked to other thematic codes	Racism, Speech, Power, Low Attendance

Once this first code has undergone the second cycle of axial coding, the researcher looks to 'saturate' the code with the remaining codes within the thematic category. Saturation occurs when a pattern of argument emerges and 'no new properties, dimensions, conditions, actions or consequences are seen in the data.'[35]

Through axial coding methodology, it is possible to identify the connected themes of speech, power (that is judgment on appropriate behaviour) and racism. The code and thick description above show that terms of expression offered by Black Nigerian members are seen as 'different and very forward' in comparison to the Black Jamaican minister and the White British secretary who would 'probably say the same thing' but in a more 'diplomatic' manner. Certain types of expression are judged to be appropriate for the Church Meeting based on 'cultural' forms of speech. Therefore, this project data suggests that in multi-ethnic

---

[35] Anselm Strauss and Juliet Corbin, *Basics of Qualitative Research: Techniques and procedures for developing grounded theory* (2nd Ed., London: Sage, 1998), 136.

churches, the Church Meeting encounters power struggles and racism which are seen in a lack of acceptance of different terms of expression or speech.

The following example expands the connections between speech, power and racism to also include a rejection of African theology. Coleman Baptist is a large evangelical charismatic church in the heart of a busy town. I observed the AGM with the expectation that it would be equivalent to my experience of being a minister in another similar church. At my previous church, the AGM would always generate multiple queries regarding finance and approval of the budget. Therefore, I was surprised that no questions at all were asked of the budget even though it was ambitious and based on a substantial increase in giving from members. When I asked the minister about the lack of questions about the finance presentation to the AGM, Carol told me of a history of difficulties with finance causing conflict at the Church Meeting. I was told the story of the previous treasurer as:

> African and bringing the storehouses, give-give-give, tithe-tithe-tithe and it was kinda hard. And then she didn't present well, so what happened in the end was I had to kinda say to her that its good for [another deacon] to present instead.

Carol identifies differences between the previous treasurer and the general view of the Church Meeting relating to finances. She contrasts the church's general view on finances with the view shared by the treasurer as African. It is important to note that

Coleman is a multi-ethnic church, but Carol shared that Black members rarely attend the Church Meeting. In particular, she highlights the treasurer's approach of applying biblical principles like tithing and the use of the Old Testament image of filling storehouses (Malachi 3:7–12) directly into the present day. A strong emphasis on tithing can indicate a link to prosperity theology, which grew from a Pentecostal base and is now a present and popular theme in large American non-denominational churches who broadcast and publish widely. Kate Bowler argues that it rests upon four themes of faith, wealth, health and victory granted to individuals and churches who offer gifts and tithes in order to be blessed.[36] At Hedger Baptist, it was the differences of expression that were rejected by the Church Meeting, however at Colman, it was both differences in expression and theology identified as African by Carol which caused significant issues in the Church Meeting.

The Black female treasurer's presentation, speech and theology jarred with the expectations of the majority White British

---

[36] Kate Bowler *Blessed: A History of the American prosperity gospel* (New York: Oxford University Press, 2013), 7. Similar theologies are explored by Samantha Miller who traces a connection between John Chrysostom and modern African Charismatic Theology whereby prosperity is a sign of blessing for which a Christian should tithe 'because you love Him', Samantha L. Miller, *John Chrysostom and African Charismatic Theology in Conversation: Salvation, Deliverance, and the Prosperity Gospel* (Lanham, MY: Lexington, 2021), 175. Popular pastors and prolific authors such as RT Kendall and Joel Osteen have also promoted tithing as a sign of faithfulness for Christians. See RT Kendall, *Tithing*, (London: Hodder and Stoughton, 1984) and Joel Osteen, *Your Best Life now* (Brentwood, TN: FaithWords, 2004).

members who attend the Church Meeting. The minister's solution was to replace the treasurer with a different person (a White British man) for presentations at Church Meetings. Ultimately the treasurer left the church entirely and the finances are now discussed at a separate meeting outside of the Church Meeting. The role of treasurer within a Baptist church is a critical one, as an elected officer responsible as a trustee and officer to oversee the budget and production of accounts to the members at Church Meetings and at the AGM. Colman Baptist entrusted this responsibility to a Black woman but when her presentation challenged the status quo of the congregation she was put at the margins of the church again. The treasurer was simply too different in speech, ethnicity and theology for the Meeting to accept.

Power at the Church Meeting

Speech rejected by the Church Meeting is connected to the theme of power. At Hedger, the use of power is seen when speech patterns are judged as diplomatic or not. While at Coleman, power was used to determine who could present financial information and what theological viewpoint would be acceptable. Linbert Spencer as a member of the Salvation Army reflects on the experience of difference in churches and organisations:

Although most organisations say that they want individuals to bring different and innovative approaches, in practice they operate on the basis that difference is of little or no value and similarity is of great importance. This is usually not conscious or deliberate, but unless deliberate and positive action is taken to recognise, acknowledge, and promote the value of diversity, then the old order will prevail.[37]

Despite the major financial challenges facing both churches, as Spencer suggests, the 'old order' failed to hear Black and Brown members' contributions at the Church Meeting. As Jill Marsh writes: 'the crucial factor in healthy development of ethnically diverse congregations is the willingness to share power and thus, to allow the whole body to be changed by members who are seen as "other" and "different".'[38] Lorraine Dixon states that the reality of racism in our churches is about looking at the church, and where necessary to:

> highlight how Black and Asian church members are made invisible in our churches and kept on the margins. It is also about looking honestly at how our spirituality and theology can be tools that maintain the racial status quo in our churches.[39]

At both Hedger and Coleman Baptist churches, Black members who spoke in different forms of speech or shared different theological viewpoints were rejected by the Church Meeting. If the Church Meeting is to express the fullness of the Spirit through

---

[37] Spencer, *Building a Multi-ethnic Church*, 92.

[38] Jill Marsh, 'Towards an ethnically diverse British Methodist Church', *Holiness, The Journal of Wesley House Cambridge* 2.1 (2016), 24.

[39] Dixon, 'bell hooks: Teller of Truth and Dreamer of Dreams', 126.

every member participating, then the necessary work of sharing power is required. For Baptists, I argue that the rejection of members' speech and theological views that seems different to those held by the majority of members, denies the Church Meeting its potential as the priesthood of all believers to discern the mind of Christ. Axial coding links causes to consequences and has generated the connection between different forms of speech and ethnicity. Therefore, as Dixon states above, it is necessary to understand in a greater depth how the 'racial status quo' is maintained in the Church Meeting. For this I turn to Willie Jennings provides an analysis of racism within an institution.

Affection and Design of the Church Meeting

Willie Jennings is a Black American Baptist minister now Associate Professor at Yale University. His insight into the structural nature of racism explored above provides a lens to analyse further the design and deep-seated values of the Baptist Church Meeting. Using the example of the design of theological education provided by Jennings, I argue that Black speech was rejected at the Church Meeting because it is not held in affection by the historic White majority of members and fails to fit the design of the Church Meeting.

Jennings presents a practical theological analysis of theological education in *After Whiteness* that draws together themes from his previous historically based work *The Christian Imagination*.[40]

---

[40] Willie James Jennings, *The Christian Imagination: Theology and the*

Throughout *After Whiteness*, he proposes that the aim of theological education is the production of the 'self-sufficient man', a concept which is rooted in the system and structure of colonial Christianity.[41] The self-sufficient man is an image of perfect student which all other students are trained for and assessed against. For example, in the theological academy, the self-sufficient man is found to be one who has a command of ancient languages and has undergone the rigour of a theological training offered only in Europe.[42] Evidence for the self-sufficient man is found, Jennings argues, in fragments of exchange, design (of courses and assessment), building through institutions and practices, the motions of the daily life of the institution and the erotic (bodily) power of Whiteness. In particular, Jennings highlights the area of design of education that has affections for European values above all else:

As white colonial settlers built their worlds, they pulled native peoples into their world of aesthetic evaluation, connecting wide varieties of people across vast distances in a shared judgement not endemic to their forms of life. Together they would be taught what a beautiful dress looks like, the difference between good and bad wine, what are a good cigar, a proper pair of shoes, classic clothing, proper speech, correct writing … and much more and all of this woven into a vision of intellectual formation and moral

---

Origins of Race (New Haven: Yale University Press, 2010).

[41] Jennings, *After Whiteness*, 29.

[42] Jennings, *After Whiteness*, 59.

development that found this white aesthetic essential for that pedagogical work.[43]

In terms of the Church Meeting, I identify similar patterns of affection in terms of speech and theological views. At Hedger, the way Black members spoke was judged as not diplomatic or not proper as Jennings might suggest. Instead, the design of the Church Meeting is for the acceptable speech patterns to be those normally used by White members. Furthermore, at Coleman, the prosperity theology viewpoint was judged to be incorrect, identified as African and therefore failed to fit the White theological aesthetic for the church. The power used by those making judgements on acceptable speech or a particular theological viewpoint created and sustains a design for a Church Meeting that prioritises European values.

Analysis to action

Jennings argues that attending to one another is one way to dismantle the power of racism within the academy. This project argues that the practice of group work at the Church Meeting enables attending or listening to one another in such a way as to bring real change. Jennings calls for change in theological education by reforming the design of education: 'we should work towards a design that aims at an attention that forms deeper habits of attending to one another and to the world around us.'[44] As

---

[43] Jennings, *After Whiteness*, 63.
[44] Jennings, *After Whiteness*, 51.

Jennings' poem expresses, attending to each other is deeper than listening:

> I will listen, but I am not hear
> You will speak, but you are not here-ing
> You here me – putting me in my place
> But this is not my place, it belongs to
> Those not wanting escape, me
> I am gone, my inside outside already
> Searching to hear where I am heard
> As I listen.[45]

Attending to one another for Jennings is to offer an intellectual affection that is 'open toward more intense listening and learning from one another.'[46] As a practical theology project, I identify a model of group work to enable attentive listening to one another. The concept of slow wisdom as a positive Baptist practice of discernment for the Church Meeting includes the critical role of listening to others who are present in discernment.

Daniel is a middle-aged Black deacon at Gates Baptist Church. He is an ATM systems engineer, originally from Cameroon and, he added, from 'the English-speaking part'. Regarding what would make for a good Church Meeting, he cited an experience of discussing pastoral care:

---

[45] Jennings, *After Whiteness*, 72-73.
[46] Jennings, *After Whiteness*, 67.

Daniel: What I think would make a good Church Meeting, I think, is like a meeting we had where we put people into groups of four, five, six and be able to get almost everyone's views.

Ruth: Yeah-

Daniel: To give their opinion, to talk in a small group because if I'm writing down the point, you also want to contribute.

Ruth: of course-

Daniel: 'What do you think we can do?' and then we ask in that quiet mood. People will talk. There was one that we did on pastoral care that one was beautiful. So many contributions. So when we break people up in groups like that and get almost everyone's view and then we pray together. So that is, that's what I think that question on discernment will come in. We are discerning the mind of Christ on that particular point we're looking at. And then before the chairman will gather all the points and let all of us pray again on it.

Daniel identified a good meeting to be one where opinions are written down, recognized and many members contribute. He describes the discernment process as 'beautiful' because it had so many 'contributions' and a shared process of prayer. I argue that Daniel's small group work model of listening demonstrates slow wisdom. It points towards a new kind of Church Meeting with a new design where listening is intentional and operates to subvert judgements on appropriate speech or theology. Indeed, the minister at Gates uses group work as a way of transforming a Church Meeting that was historically combative. Furthermore, Stephen Holmes argues that the Church Meeting offers a radical model of transformation as it is:

> profoundly subversive of almost every human social order
> . . . This is the church, where every social division is
> levelled and each person granted the dignity of one made
> in the image of God and remade through the sacrifice of
> Christ and the work of the Spirit.[47]

A Church Meeting can begin to subvert power structures is to use the effective listening method of group work. Small group work enables members to explore differences of opinion, theology and expression. This listening approach affirms the dignity of members as created in the image of God as suggested by Holmes. The project data indicates that members are empowered through listening to each other and being heard at the Church Meeting. The process identified by this project of slow wisdom recognises that listening in such ways takes time, but this slowness helps the discernment process. Daniel at Gates Baptist Church shared an

---

[47] Stephen R. Holmes, 'Knowing the mind of Christ: Congregational government and the church meeting'. In *Questions of Identity: Studies in Honour of Brian Haymes* edited by Anthony Cross and Ruth Gouldbourne (Oxford: Regent's Park College, 2011), 185.

example of good practice that welcomed difference and actively sought a multi-voiced approach through group work. Small group work offers a way of listening to others that helps Baptists to critically discern the mind of Christ as a form of slow wisdom.

Using intersectional analysis within a qualitative research project has given greater scope to my reflection on Church Meeting practice. It holds in tension demographic changes in neighbourhoods, experiences of racism, issues of power in Baptist discernment processes and my own privilege of Whiteness as a researcher. Jennings provides a key example of the design and affections of an educational institution formed by European values above all else. His critique sheds light on the Baptist Church Meeting where there may be preferred terms of speech or theology and little room for difference. I argue from the project data that group work which carefully helps each person to express their opinion offers one way for differences to be shared and explored at a Church Meeting. Here the Baptist practice of listening to each other provides space in which a radical model of empowerment can be used. Listening and attending to different voices at the Church Meeting is critical to discernment, to the practice of slow wisdom and to the vitality of the Baptist church as the priesthood of all believers.

2 Bread, Jerk Chicken, Wine, and Whisky: New Food at the Lord's Table

Simon Jay

Story – A Strange New Meal

My first experience with the Eucharist meal was when I was 12 years old. I had started going to a growing independent church that met in a chapel building in Somerset. I had found out about the Church from a Christian youth club that I had recently begun to attend. That Sunday evening, I made the journey by myself to the church and arrived sometime after the service had started. As I walked through the door, I became aware that I had absolutely no idea what I was supposed to do. It had not occurred to me that the space that I was entering would require a certain understanding of the rules, rituals, and behaviour codes. Questions like, 'where do I sit, how loud can I speak, what if I need the toilet?' were a concern for me. It was not until I caught the eye of one of my friends sitting in the third row from the back that I began to become less panicky. He had saved me a seat, and I shuffled through the row and joined the group of other young people that I also knew from the youth club.

I had probably been sitting there about 20 minutes when someone from the front stood up and began a ritual that I thought was so strange and peculiar. The whole room instantly fell into some sort

29

of sombre silence. It was like he flicked a switch, and everyone knew what that meant except me. All I knew, judging by the intense silence and sombre-looking faces, was that this was serious stuff. The man at the front was ripping a large loaf of bread into pieces whilst uttering words about broken bodies, blood, sin, and forgiveness. Although I had little understanding of what he was talking about, at that point, I was feeling relatively comfortable. Then something happened that terrified me. He put the bread on a plate, poured wine in a cup and started passing it down the rows where people began eating and drinking it. Just a small bit of bread and a tiny sip of wine were consumed from the plate and cup. Some of them would have their eyes closed, most of them would mumble something before consuming the bread and wine, and often, they would put their hands on their neighbours' shoulders and whisper something in their ears. All this was done in relative silence. However, what was most terrifying was that the bread and wine were coming in my direction. As I try to recall the memory of this experience, I can't recollect eating the bread. All I can remember is receiving a metal cup full of wine and a napkin. I had no idea what to do. How much should I drink? Was I even allowed to drink it, and what were the right words I needed to say? So, as I put the cup to my mouth, with all of these doubts and indecisions in my mind, I took a sip and made a great slurp sound that ripped through the silence. At that moment, the entire youth group that I was sitting with burst into uncontrollable laughter. This worked out pretty well for me, as not only did it break the tension that I was feeling, but it also actually increased my popularity with the other young people. I was the kid who slurped the blood of Jesus.

Now, over the years, I have learnt and become very comfortable with the various rituals that surround the Eucharist. I would be happy and confident walking into most churches and participating in this meal. This is only because I have had to disassociate this meal from my everyday cultural practices and adopt another set of foreign practices that have no correlation to how my current community celebrates, laments and experiences life. It is, therefore, that I unapologetically want to argue for new and more inclusive practices, for what Noel Moules suggests is the only physical thing that Jesus gave us to build his church.[48] My Baptist identity encourages me to contextualise my practices and theology and draw on the experiences of my local setting. So, as I reflect on this meal, I not only want to suggest that we can have different foods at the table, but I also want to argue that we can partake in this meal in different places and radical spaces.

A New Setting for the Meal

One of the cornerstones of our Baptist identity is our commitment to share a simple meal together.[49] A meal situated around a table of bread and wine. It is in this gathered space we trust that, as a community of believers, we encounter the risen Christ. However, this meal, which Nigel Scotland reminds us, began its roots in the

---

[48] Noel Moules, *Fingerprints of Fire: Footprints of Peace: A Spiritual Manifesto from a Jesus Perspective*. (Winchester: Circle, 2012), 164.

[49] For an account of Baptists and the Lord Supper, see Christopher J. Ellis, *Gathering* (London: SCM, 2004), 176-99.

day-to-day life of the community,[50] and can often feel ritualised and disconnected from the lived experiences of the people sharing it.

This chapter is set in my neighbourhood, which is located in the city of Birmingham and starts with our arrival back in 2000. My wife and I intentionally moved into the neighbourhood as part of a local Church of England church plant. At that time, we understood our role as missionaries, and our aim was to help support the newly developed church plant that met at the local primary school. There was much talk about the neighbourhood's bad reputation, and I remember a year earlier listening to the Parish vicar for the area sharing heroic stories from his newly published book at a Churches Together event. He told how God had sent angels to sit on the walls of the vicarage to protect his family and the church members from the immoral, wicked, and often-violent behaviour of the local 'thugs'.[51] I recall at the end of the service how many people exclaimed how brave this vicar and his church must be. Even at this stage, this narrative that was coming from the 'white middle class' Christian leaders about this culturally diverse neighbourhood did not sit comfortably with us.

---

[50] Nigel Scotland, *The New Passover: Rethinking the Lord's Supper for Today* (Eugene, OR: Cascade, 2016). In his book Nigel refers to the different kinds and names of meals that the early Christians would regularly have. He is constantly connecting the meals to the already recognised everyday meals that were being eaten.

[51] Wallace Brown and Mary Brown, *Angels on the Wall* (Eastbourne: Kingsway, 2000).

Such narratives about the community could be considered as a form of signification that both Gates and Long explore.[52]

However, when we arrived in the neighbourhood, we were immediately struck by how different this community felt compared to the narrative that was told in the book. Rather than being confronted by crime and anti-social behaviour, my wife and I were overwhelmed by the generous hospitality that we were shown. Food and drink seemed ever-flowing, and I can recall countless occasions when we were invited into people's houses to join in with their families' meals. Each of these meals had its own cultural practices, and learning the various codes was both fun and problematic. On one particular occasion, we were invited to share a meal with a Muslim Eritrean and Ethiopian family. The mum brought out small dishes filled with food and then handed us a plate that had Injera Ethiopian flatbread on it. She instructed us to scoop the food from the bowls onto the flatbread and eat it with our hands. After devouring all of the food from my plate she quickly left and went to the kitchen. Feeling nicely full I was slightly concerned when she came back with more bread and dishes. In order to be polite and not offend, my wife and I began tucking into the second course and just about managed to finish it. It was not until the third course of food was brought to us that

---

[52] Henry Louis Gates, Jr., *The Signifying Monkey: A Theory of African American Literary Criticism* (Oxford: Oxford University Press, 2014); Charles H. Long, *Significations: Signs, Symbols, and images in the interpretation of Religion* (Colorado: Fortress, 1986). Both these authors explore this idea of how we 'Signify' upon different people or things. This can often be a way of projecting false narratives on people to 'goad' them.

her son leaned over and told us 'Mum will keep filling your plates if you keep clearing them'. That night, we learnt that we were inadvertently being rude by eating everything on our plates. She would have understood this action as a sign that we were still hungry, and this would have made her feel like a bad hostess. Whereas we were taught clearing one's plate is polite, in her culture, it is respectful to leave food as a sign that one is well-fed and satisfied. Although this story illustrates the cultural nuances around our meal tables, it also acts as a problematic discourse of how we understand the spaces in which we partake in the Eucharist meal.

Bringing Another Story to the Table

Within this new space where we found ourselves, we quickly recognised that many of the stories that we heard were strange and foreign to us. For the past 30 years, my Christian journey had understood the Biblical stories in what I would argue was a White Western context. Although I myself am a Black man, I had learnt to assimilate within my exclusively white Christian communities and hence created my story of faith that fitted with my current Western values and ideals. As I thought about this new community, a community with its diversity of culture, ethnicity, and language, I became uneasy with transposing much of my theology onto that place. This was no different to my thinking and understanding of the Eucharist. I had come to the conclusion that most Eucharistic meals that I attended told a story that nicely fitted into a White Western narrative. I am aware that this can be a very challenging statement, but I ask you to bear with me.

The story of Israel's liberation from Egypt has been taught to many Christians in our Churches. The Jewish community remembers this story each week during the Passover meal, and their holy book clearly outlines the preparations and rituals that need to take place before eating this meal. As the Jewish community gathers around the table, they have prepared themselves, the food, their houses, and their hearts in order to remember their epic journey of slavery to liberation. We are told of how Jesus took the bread and broke it, drawing from this ancient story that had been passed down throughout the generations in the Passover meal. At the Last Supper, he gave new meaning to this meal, which continued the tradition of breaking bread and drinking wine within the early Christian communities. Although it has taken on several names, communion, breaking of bread and wine, The Lord's Supper, etc., this tradition has been consistently practised throughout the centuries and is still a core sacrament for the church today. However, during most of the services that I have attended, the emphasis has been on our individual freedom. This has often been associated with freedom from sin and death. I have very rarely been in a service that has connected this meal with historical events of slavery and liberation. An interesting question that we could ask ourselves is this one. Have we formed this emphasis on our individual liberation because, for most of us, we do not have a history of slavery and oppression? To ask yet another question, how do we make sense of liberation if our own historical stories point the finger at us as the oppressors?

It is my experience that the way we understand and construct this meal within our Western Christian traditions draws very little from the stories of oppressed people. Given the roots of the meal, this could be seen as extremely surprising. I would therefore like to intentionally story this meal around a people group, who, like the Israelites, have known captivity and slavery and yet still today are praying for liberation from their slave masters.

Story — Preparing the Meal for the Lord's Table

I remember my first introduction to preparing and cooking Jerk chicken. We had made a conscious decision at the Haven Centre to ensure that the food we offered was representative of the different cultures in our community. So, when I was approached by a couple of local Caribbean Women who offered to take me under their wing and teach me the art of cooking Caribbean dishes, I metaphorically 'bit their hands off'.

I had come prepared with pen and paper and was studiously writing everything down. In my mind, I was hoping to end up with a precise recipe that was neatly ordered alongside the methodology. It was not long before I realised that cooking Caribbean food was something that could not easily be logged and put into a recipe book. Cooking Caribbean food was part of these women's DNA. The art of cooking has been passed down through the generations.

The women began putting the ingredients on the chopping boards. Out came the ginger, Scotch Bonnet chilli peppers, thyme, garlic, spring onions and pimento seeds. These were all carefully chopped, crushed, and mixed with some all-purpose seasoning, brown sugar and soya sauce to make a spicy paste. The women did not measure out by weight; they simply used their eyes and tasted the sauce to check if a little more thyme was needed or another clove of garlic.

As the preparation continued, I noticed something profound happening to the space. Conversation started to take form. This was no longer just a kitchen but a place to share stories, a place to laugh so much one began to cry, a place to lament as we talked about our worries and fears and a place to pray to a God who understood what is like to be marginalised, persecuted, and ultimately put to death by the authorities. As a Black man, I found myself being drawn into these conversations. We talked often about our own experiences of racism as well as the institutional racism that our children were subject to in their schools, colleges, and society. We dreamed dreams together and told new stories of liberation and hope for us and our children. The seasoning that we had made spoke into our stories and experiences. The fiery spices of the chilli and ginger mixed with the sweet taste of the sugar somehow resonated with the often-painful struggles of our everyday lives as we wait for that sweet day when Jesus will wipe away all racism and comfort all those who mourn. This was not simply a space for preparing food; it was a space to talk into being the 'Kingdom of Heaven'.

I noticed a practice that went against our Western food hygiene training.[53] During the preparation, everything was washed. Bowls were filled up with water, and substantial quantities of vinegar were added. The women would then spend over an hour cleaning and washing the chicken, cutting off all that undesirable fat, gristle, and bone. I recall one of the washers saying, 'we are washing away hundreds of years of slavery and oppression.'

The freshly seasoned chicken would then be put into the fridge to marinate overnight. The longer the marinating period, the more time the seasoning would have to soak into the meat, enabling the flavours to go deep into the food. The preparation of this meal could not be rushed. Time was needed to allow it to mature, and I had the strong sense that when one comes to eat it, they are not simply eating chicken but participating in the Afro-Caribbean story of slavery and oppression that goes back over 400 years.

Holding Space Together

The preparation for this Eucharist meal was part of the everyday preparation of food that many of these Caribbean women would be doing. Theologians, such as Nigel Scotland, who have explored in depth the diversity and development of the meal within the early church, strongly argue for this meal being

---

[53] Food hygiene recommendations state that meat should not be washed but either immediately be put in the fridge/freezer or the oven/BBQ to be cooked. This always creates an element of tension between the Food Hygiene trainer and our volunteers during the course.

integrated into the everyday lives of the community.[54] The idea of separating it from the other meals and turning it into a liturgical ritual came later, and I would agree with Scotland's assertions that this meal is best placed as part of our everyday family and community meals. Food is a central element in all of our community gatherings. The food that is served always represents the cultures of the people that are preparing the meal. The drinks of choice are rum-punch or whisky within the Caribbean community in my neighbourhood. It wouldn't be a celebration, whether it be a wedding, a child's blessing, or a birthday, without curry mutton, chicken, fish and rice. If you are looking for cheese sandwiches or quiches, you will be disappointed. This richness of tradition and cooking creates a fantastic space for the community to get together as they prepare for the upcoming celebration.

During the preparation of the meal at the Haven Centre, the act of holding space together was central. This practice was common within the everyday rhythms of the early Christians. They would regularly come together within their homes to share food and break bread (Acts 2:42-47). According to John Koenig, it is this 'Koinonia' that takes place as an act of shared worship.[55] Other theologians, such as Scotland, also highlight how important this act of holding space together was for the early Christian, and I go

---

[54] Scotland, *The New Passover*.

[55] John Koenig, *New Testament Hospitality: Partnership with Strangers as Promise and Mission* (Eugene, OR: Wipf and Stock, 2001), 9.

along with William Barclay's assertion that *koinonia* is not simply a meeting or gathering but 'a sharing of friendship.'[56]

It was during the preparation of the meal at the Haven Centre that I found this friendship and connectivity. More than this, something powerfully subversive was at play. The space that they had created seemed counter to what is often my experience when my colleagues or I are preparing for our church gatherings. I frequently set aside a definitive amount of time, shut myself in a room and turn off my phone. This is all done to minimise any distractions that might prevent the flow of productivity. It was very clear in the preparation of this Eucharistic gathering at the Haven that the priorities were not centred on how productive we could be, but rather, the focus was on the rich conversation and connection that happened in the time that we spent together.

A challenge for me, as I have worked with the Caribbean community, has often been this tension between a Western value of time and productivity and the perception that many Black communities seem ambiguous in their timekeeping. As I reflected on some of these tensions within our gathered spaces, my explorations were enriched during an online seminar I attended in October 2020. It was titled, 'Why we need Black Radicalism'. One of the speakers challenged this idea of timekeeping, stating that the way the West prioritises time is due to the values that it puts on productivity and capitalism. The speaker went on to state

---

[56] William Barclay, *New Testament Word Book* (London: SCM, 1955), 71-72 cited in Scotland, *The New Passover*, 63.

that time is constructed as an oppressive mechanism that prevents Black people from 'holding space' with one another and reimagining a new future for themselves. As we explored this idea more, I became increasingly excited about the implications that this could have for my community and the way in which we gather. We have to take seriously the possibility that many of our church services are so ordered that they leave very little space for *koinonia* and the sharing of deep and intimate friendships. I am wholly convinced that the gatherings of the newly formed Christian communities would have been more akin to the Caribbean community and the way they prepared the chicken at the Haven Centre than many of my experiences during the Eucharist services in the church.

The Cross and the Lynching Tree

I want to touch on the richness of conversation that emerged within the space as we prepared the food for our Eucharist meal. I have talked about a *koinonia* space and a subversive space. Now, I want to turn our attention to a broken space. As the dialogue developed, we found ourselves holding such a space, a space of brokenness. It was not long before the chatter steered towards the suffering and oppression that everyone felt. I have been in many church services where we are given the length of a song to prepare ourselves to encounter the crucified Christ at the Lord's Table. During the preparation of this meal, we took time to stand in that place of brokenness and reflect on the person of Jesus, looking like a young black man hanging from a tree with a rope around his neck.

The conversation was deepened by stories not just from the present but stories that went back generations that spoke of slavery from the past. The feeling of abandonment was ever-present as we talked together. James Cone is uncompromising when relating the lived experience of Black people with the cross of Jesus. In his book *The Cross and the Lynching Tree*, Cone narrates many stories of Black people who had ropes tied around their necks as they hung from trees. This all takes place in front of a lynch mob screaming and shouting their approval at the execution. 'Like Jesus, blacks knew torture and abandonment, with no community or government capable or willing to protect them from the crazed mobs.'[57] Unlike the Israelites' journey of liberation from Egypt, the Black community then, and still now, have never entered the Promised Land. When the images in May 2020 of George Floyd being crushed to death under the knee of the authorities appeared on our screens, it served as a vivid reminder of the stark reality that the violence and oppression against Black people is still present today.

As we talked together, there was recognition of the deep trauma that each one felt, not only thinking about the everyday struggles as we attempted to hold space in a world entrenched with institutionalised racism but also as we reflected on the history of the horrors that Black people have been subject to over the past 400 years. Yet remarkably, we held this profound wound up

---

[57] James H. Cone, *The Cross and the Lynching Tree* (New York: Orbis, 2013), 75.

towards the Heavens. As Cone puts it, 'Black faith emerged out of black people's wrestling with suffering, the struggle to make sense out of their senseless situation, as they relate their own predicament to similar stories in the Bible.'[58] We recognised a theology, which is very seldom taught in our churches, where the crucified Christ inhabits the bodies of our Black brothers and sisters as they hang from the lynching tree. Cone writes about the wishes of Mamie Till Bradley, the mother of 14-year-old Emmett Till, who got lynched on August 24th, 1955, for reportedly whistling at a White woman and saying, "bye Baby." When his body was brought back, she wanted him to have an open casket so that 'everybody can see what they did to my boy.'[59] Cone goes on to say that 'She exposed white brutality and Black faith to the world, significantly, exposed a parallel meaning between her son's lynching and the crucifixion of Jesus.'[60] She refused to accept that his life was sacrificed in vain but rather pleaded to God that he would use her son's death to prevent other young Black people from getting lynched.

The stories that we told as we prepared ourselves and the food for the Eucharist meal at the Haven, were stories that echoed a history of slavery, oppression and executions, the effects that still keep our community in bondage today. I have never been more aware of the relevance and power of the cross as we allowed the Crucified Christ to inhabit our history. At the Lord's table, we

---

[58] Cone, *Cross and the Lynching Tree*, 124.
[59] Cone, *Cross and the Lynching Tree*, 66.
[60] Cone, *Cross and the Lynching Tree*, 67.

have this hope. The weakness and brokenness of Jesus can be seen in the lived experiences and history of an enslaved community. It is in this brokenness that we find our hope and salvation for the whole world.

I am further heartened by Belier's exploration of this hope, not just for our salvation but also for the wider world. She states that 'In the Eucharist we participate in the body of the risen Christ, seeking redemption for our own bodies, our communities, and the global body of the planet earth'.[61] She goes on to say that 'when we come together at the table, we engage in the work of lifting up the groaning of creation . . . We remind God of the suffering of concrete bodies; we give voice to those who are not heard in the public square.'[62] This meal can simultaneously hold the violence and oppression of the years of slavery and racism whilst looking forward to a future hope and a promise that the day will come when all racism, injustice and humiliation will be washed away.

Purity and Cleanliness

Before I continue, I want to leave you with the image of the ritual of washing our food as we prepare for the meal. I cannot express how ingrained this ritual is amongst the members of our Caribbean community and the deep correlation between our conversations about slavery and the act of washing our chicken as

---

[61] Andrea Bieler and Luise Schottroff, *The Eucharist: Bodies, Bread, & Resurrection* (Minneapolis: Fortress, 2007), 3.

[62] Bieler and Schottroff, *Eucharist*, 7.

part of the preparation process. 'We are washing away hundreds of years of racism and oppression.'

As I reflected on the stories and experiences of the Caribbean community, I became convinced of the importance of incorporating the ritual of washing the food within the Eucharist meal. This ritual resonates with the 'crucified Christ' and ensures that the injustices and shame of the cross are not forgotten. The Eucharist is not a static liturgical practice but rather a meal that interacts with the injustices and brokenness of people's lived realities. It was clear that this community profoundly felt the effects of hundreds of years of racial oppression. The recognition of this as a central part of the meal, enacted out through the ritual of washing the food, enables the broken Christ to stand in solidarity with a community who have been subjected to horrendous acts of violence, oppression, and slavery.

Story – Jerk Chicken and Whisky

This particular Saturday evening, I knew I was going into a space that would profoundly challenge my assumptions, values, and theology. Earlier that week, I had asked Cool J, a middle-aged Jamaican gentleman, if I could share a Eucharistic meal with him. I explained the Christian practice of breaking bread and drinking wine together as a way of connecting with the Easter story. His response was, "we don't drink wine, you better be bringing whisky instead, and whilst we are eating, I will be doing some Jerk Chicken." So, as I was making my way to his home, excited about the Jerk Chicken and carrying a bottle of whisky, I got a phone call from Cool J saying, "and make sure you pick up some cigarettes on the way." I stood outside his door and prayed. A simple prayer, "God be with me in this place tonight.' I will admit I was a little bit anxious. When I entered his flat, Cool J took me to one side and told me, "we are bad people here, I don't want you to compromise yourself and become like us." It was important for him that I stayed integral to who I was, as he considered the environment that I was entering to be ungodly and unwholesome.

There were several other people in the flat, and we spent the evening drinking whisky, eating Jerk Chicken, and smoking cigarettes. We talked about some profound and deep issues that centred on identity, race, spirituality, faith, power, and White space. Cool J asked me, "do you see how many White people are in my flat tonight?" The answer was none. "In over 12 years that I have lived here there has not been one single White person in my flat other than the police, and they are not invited."

We discussed institutional racism, particularly within the church. 'Christianity is a White man's religion used to justify slavery and oppression to Black people,' he would say. As we explored these issues, I asked him this question, 'For you to give Jesus any consideration at all what would need to change?' He said, 'He would need to be Black'. As we talked, ate, drank, and smoked cigarettes together, something profound began to happen. I was struck by the continued presence of God that I felt in his flat, and over this Eucharistic meal, a seeing of each other occurred. At the end of the evening, Cool J embraced me and gave thanks to the

God that he saw in me. As we held each other, I felt the embrace of Jesus.

Hospitality from the Margins

At the beginning of this chapter, I gave a description of the first Eucharist meal that I attended. I guess it's fair to suggest that as a young Black person entering a church that had an exclusively White congregation, I could be considered as a marginal person coming to the centre. I was entering a civilised space, a space that had particular purity rituals and behaviour codes that I would quickly have to learn if I wanted to 'fit in' or be accepted. In order not to be excluded from such spaces, Miroslav Volf explores the process of assimilation as a way of 'fitting in.'[63] Although I was desperately trying to find out how I should act in this strange space (assimilate), from the church's point of view, there was an issue of contamination at stake. What I mean by this is to say that the church service needed to be conducted in a certain way with certain expected behaviours from the members of the congregation. To push the point further, it is worth exploring Neyrey's understanding of purity maps in the New Testament. These New Testament purity maps are a means to justify the separation between objects, people, and places, amongst other things.[64] This can be seen when thinking about the Jewish

---

[63] Miroslav Volf, *Exclusion and Embrace: A theological Exploration of Identity, Otherness, and Reconciliation* (Nashville: Abingdon, 1996), 67.

[64] Jerome Neyrey, *Paul, In Other Words: A Cultural Reading of His Letters* (Louisville, KY: Westminster/John Knox, 1990), 27-30.

understanding of place. They would have understood that 'Israel was set apart from all other lands; and so, it sat at the centre of any map and place that mattered.'[65] So, how do we understand this in the context of Cool J and his house? I would like to make some correlation between this theological understanding of centeredness within Jewish thought and our understanding of the centeredness within our church buildings.

Returning to the Eucharist meal in that small chapel in Somerset, I will hypothetically relocate my encounter with Cool J from his flat and place it in that church service. I can already begin to feel myself tense up as some obvious problems begin to emerge. I hear his voice below out, "We don't drink wine we drink whisky . . . and while you are at it bring some cigarettes." We do not have to stretch our imaginations very far to deduce that people gulping back whisky whilst taking a drag of a cigarette before passing it along the aisle would be deeply problematic for most members of our congregations. The sacredness and purity of the space would be considered contaminated. Don't misunderstand me; I am not advocating that we pass down cigarettes and whisky in order to make our Eucharist meals more inclusive. I am highlighting the point that we may have to resign ourselves to the thought that not all are welcome to the table. That is if our table is in our space.

So, where do we go from here? I believe that stories of hospitality in the biblical narrative can assist us in this. In order for us to bridge these two worlds, I am going to lightly touch on some of

---

[65] Neyrey, *Paul, In Other Words*, 49.

the examples of hospitality that are visible in the Bible. In Luke, we read a story about a woman from the city, a sinner, who took care of Jesus by washing his weary feet with expensive ointment and drying them with her hair (Luke 7:37-38). Again, we read about another woman who drew water from a well to give to Jesus so that he could quench his thirst (John 4:6-8). On another occasion, he invited himself to Zacchaeus' house and allowed himself to be hosted by yet another 'sinner' (Luke 19:5). It appears to me that on many of these occasions, the hosts do not find themselves at the 'Centre.' On the contrary, our Biblical hosts find themselves often marginalised, described as 'sinners' and thought of as being unclean, unholy, and profane. Like my friend Cool J, there is a risk that these marginal hosts will contaminate the purity of the religious and holy spaces. It is, therefore, my suggestion that if we are serious about sending out the invitation to the highways and byways to those on the margins, then we need to move away from our centres that we consider sacred and pure. We may be surprised at what we discover if we inhabit the space of the 'other' and allow ourselves to be served by a marginal host. There are obvious dangers as such a move can often leave us vulnerable and unsure, as was felt by my wife and I as we ate a meal at the house of our Eritrean and Ethiopian friends. However, it is only when we move out of our centred spaces that that which was once considered impure and profane can find a place at the Lord's table. It is in these spaces that we discover those who were once invisible are now made visible. In the gospel of Luke, Simon and his guests could only see a sinner (Luke 7:39), but as she tended to the needs of Jesus, a truer seeing of this woman was revealed whilst simultaneously exposing the blindness of those sitting around him.

> Do you see this woman? I entered your house; you gave me no water for my feet, but she has bathed my feet with her tears and dried them with her hair. You gave me no kiss, but from the time I came in she has not stopped kissing my feet. You did not anoint my head with oil, but she has anointed my feet with ointment. Therefore, I tell you, her sins, which were many, have been forgiven; hence she has shown great love. But the one to whom little is forgiven, loves little (Luke 7: 44-47).

We continue to see this reconfiguration of space in Eric Clark Stewart's book *Gathered around Jesus*. Stewart suggests that 'Mark challenges both Roman and early Jewish ways of thinking about space, rejecting these 'civilised' centres and providing alternative loci for the formation of the Jesus' movement.'[66] In the very first chapter of Mark, Jesus goes to Capernaum and enters the synagogue on the Sabbath. It is here that he casts out a Demon. What was supposed to be a sacred space, Mark identifies it as a contaminated space. Infected by an unclean spirit. Stewart argues that this act from Jesus that identified unclean spirits in the synagogue was the start of a ministry that began to reconfigure civilised space. Reflecting on Stewart's reading of Mark's

---

[66] Eric Clark Stewart, *Gathered around Jesus: An Alternative Spatial Practice in the Gospel of Mark* (Eugene, OR: Cascade, 2009), 180.

Gospel, I want to suggest that civilised space is rejected and replaced with 'Jesus Space.'

Not only does 'Jesus space' help us to redefine the purity systems and how that affects who can perform in the spaces, but it also changes our spatial practices in relation to time. I would propose that this 'Jesus space' could be a transient or a 'pop up' space. It is not reliant on our planning or timing but happens when it happens. The Holy Spirit blows where he chooses (John 3:8). He is not restricted by time or place. The physical location is no longer sacred for its own sake, and therefore, purity rituals do not need to be performed to protect the space from threats or contamination.

New Food at the Lord's Table

I entitled this chapter 'New Food at the Lord's Table'. My purpose was to draw from the stories and richness of the cultures from the people in my neighbourhood and bring them to the centre of our Eucharist meal. I hope that I have shown how new liturgical practices, rhythms and food can create deep meaning, particularly for the African Caribbean culture. A culture that shares aspects of the Jewish story of diaspora, slavery, and oppression.

In writing this chapter, I am aware that some of the practices may seem to subvert hundreds of years of Baptist church tradition. However, our tradition, as it has listened to scripture, has subverted the accepted tradition, demonstrated in the way we have baptised only believers and celebrated at the Lord's Table. As

Baptists, it is this ability to be subversive that should aid us in asking big questions about our current rituals. Are they relevant in reflecting the images of Jesus within our current spaces? I would encourage us to reflect on our roots as Baptists and remember that we come from a tradition that has challenged the status quo.[67] I am not arguing that we should do this for its own sake, but I hope that I have shown that our current practices, rituals, and traditions often exclude and alienate those who are different.

Our Baptist identity gives us the freedom to ask questions not only about what food is brought to the table but also to consider the possibility that we may need to relocate our sacred meals to marginal places. The Biblical narrative often places Jesus in such marginal places as he gathers people around himself before eating a meal. We find him on the hilltops sharing bread and fish with over 5000 people. He visits Peter by the waters, where again he shares a simple meal of fish with a few of his closest friends, and I have already brought to our attention the story of Zacchaeus, a sinner who hosted and ate a meal with Jesus.

It would be tempting at this point for us to place ourselves within Jesus' position within these stories. How easy it would be for me to see myself as the divine figure inhabiting Cool J's space within his flat. On the contrary, I want to leave you with this thought. It is not myself that represents the presence of God in Cool J's space, but instead, I find that Jesus is already there. His presence resides

---

[67] See Curtis Freeman, *Undomesticated Dissent* (Waco: Baylor, 2017).

in the holy sacrament of the Eucharist. It is discovered in the preparation of the food, the richness of the ingredients and the storytelling of the oppressed and marginalised. The crucified Christ inhabits this Eucharist meal in the form of a young Black man being lynched from a tree. As I share this meal of Jerk Chicken and Whisky with my neighbours from the Caribbean community, I meet Jesus in their food, in their stories and in their history.

3 Preaching with Sick on my Shoulder: Reflections on Motherhood and Baptist Ministry

Leigh Greenwood

Motherhood and ministry are inseparable for me, so much so that as I started to draft this opening in a rare moment away from the demands of both, I found myself describing them as my twin vocations.[68] I felt compelled to pursue ministry even before I had any idea of how or where I would do it, whereas I don't feel called to motherhood in a conceptual sense so much as to be a mother to the two children I call my own, so I have been drawn to and experienced them very differently, and yet I can see that each shapes and makes sense of my life in a way that demands I take them both seriously as vocations. They also shape and make sense of one another, and I think it is this that leads me to see them as twins, each with their own character but each in constant relationship with the other. The language seems particularly appropriate given that, for me, ministry and motherhood arrived at the same time and have rarely left one another alone since.[69] I

---

[68] Are they twins or do I have triplets? Is my marriage also a vocation? Perhaps that is for another reflection.

[69] I started training for ministry in September 2015, and my son was born in June 2016. I took a short maternity leave before returning to study and placement with a three-month-old in tow. I took up my first solo pastorate in September 2018, and my daughter was born in June 2020. I took six months of maternity leave and returned to work while still a full-time carer for the baby.

simply don't know what it is to engage in either ministry or motherhood without the other because I have never experienced it; just as a mother of twins will not know how it feels to have been a parent to just one child.

In the piece that follows, I want to consider this complicated relationship between ministry and motherhood by reflecting on a handful of moments from the past seven years, from breaking the news of my first pregnancy early in my ministerial formation to preaching with sick on my shoulder to struggling to adjust to maternity leave for a second time. Our stories all have value in themselves, and so I hope that offering these snippets of my own very particular experience will serve as an encouragement and example for readers to create their own spaces for storytelling and reflection.[70] But our stories also have meaning for our shared lives, and so I will seek to reflect on the ways in which using motherhood as a model or metaphor for ministry might enrich our collective understanding and provide language and imagery for the benefit of the wider church.

Before I begin, I want to be clear that while I will draw on the reflections of others as well as my own experiences, what follows does not pretend to be a comprehensive study of either motherhood or ministry. Neither are monolithic, and no two

---

[70] Jules Middleton likewise seeks to create this space for others, ending each chapter on her book about being a ministry mum with a reflection from a fellow ministry mum. See Jules Middleton, *Breaking the Mould: Learning to Thrive as a Ministry Mum* (London: SPCK, 2020).

mothers or ministers will experience or approach them in the same way. I would also like to avoid the sort of reductive thinking that puts clear water between motherhood and fatherhood. In using 'Parent' as a model for ministry, Derek Tidball characterises "the tender mother" by affection, self-giving and gentleness, and "the model father" by individual care, teaching and modelling,[71] but this fails to adequately represent my own experience of both parenting and being parented, and leans into the 'soft binary complementarity' that Beth Allison-Glenny critiques in arguments for women's ministry.[72] There are certainly particularities to the experience of motherhood, most especially the physicalities of pregnancy and breastfeeding and the not yet completely redundant societal expectation that the mother will be the primary carer. And yet, even these are not common to all mothers, and motherhood should not be confined to or conflated with them. Many a mother has been oppressed by the expectation that she will sacrifice herself to the role, and many a father has been constricted by the assumption that he will be a figure of discipline rather than devotion, and so we need to take a more nuanced view.

It may then seem strange to write a piece reflecting on motherhood at all, and it might be argued that it would be better

---

[71] Derek Tidball, *Builders and Fools: Leadership the Bible way* (Nottingham: IVP, 1999), 91ff.

[72] Beth Allison-Glenny, 'Baptist Interpretations of Scripture on the Complementarity of Male and Female' in *Gathering Disciples* edited by Myra Blyth and Andy Goodliff (Eugene: Pickwick, 2017), 97-102.

to speak in gender-neutral terms of parenting, but we inherit certain modes of speech, and my own story has been shaped very much by the realities of bearing and nursing children, so I instinctively began with motherhood and looked to other mothers for their reflections. While I may wish to challenge some of the assumptions and associations that come with the language of mothering, they may be lost entirely if I were simply to replace every mention of motherhood with parenthood. We must start from where we are, and Emma Percy suggests that '"parenting" does not yet convey the warmth of relationship and ordinariness of "mothering", and it lacks the rich traditional resonances,'[73] although the 'yet' is hopeful that there will be a move towards a broader and subtler understanding of these terms. A comprehensive study of parenting in all its varied forms is beyond the scope of this piece, but I hope these reflections contribute to that move, and I encourage the reader to bring the nuance that will come from their own experiences to what follows.

Motherhood in Baptist Ministerial Life

I may be relatively unusual, but I am not unique in being a mother in Baptist ministry, and so before I share my own experiences, I want to give them some context by locating myself within the history of mothers in ministry in Baptist life.[74] I trust it goes

---

[73] Emma Percy, *What Clergy Do: especially when it looks like nothing* (London: SPCK, 2014), 17.

[74] Throughout this chapter, I use Baptist as shorthand to refer to the Baptist Union of Great Britain.

without saying that our identity is first and foremost as children of God, and little of what follows in this essay will be exclusively Baptist in experience or application, but I do want to show that motherhood and ministry coexist within our tradition, and therefore that reflection on the connections and intersections between them properly belongs within conversations about our shared identity.

The Baptist Union of Great Britain first recognised Women Pastors in 1922,[75] but it was nearly another half century before it experienced its first mother in ministry. Ruth Matthews was only the sixth woman to be accredited as a Baptist minister when she and her husband John were jointly called to the pastorate of Swindon Baptist Tabernacle in 1970. Their first son was born later that year, and a second followed in 1973,[76] with Ruth returning to work after each maternity leave so that she and John were both 'half-time minister and half-time parent,'[77] pioneering a new way of balancing pastorate and parenthood. Official records will not show how many female ministers following Ruth have had children while in pastoral ministry, but maternity guidelines only seem to have been produced following a campaign led by a gathering of women in ministry and training, which was founded

---

[75] Faith Bowers, 'Liberating Women for Baptist Ministry', *Baptist Quarterly* 45.8 (2014): 457.

[76] Ruth and John Matthews, 'A Husband and Wife Partnership', *The Fraternal* 192 (July 1980): 15-16.

[77] Matthews, 'A Husband and Wife Partnership', 15.

in the mid-1980s,[78] so we might reasonably suppose that there had not been sufficient numbers to warrant sooner response. A fuller document including practical and pastoral advice on pregnancy and maternity leave for ministers and churches, alongside stories of women who had recently had children in pastorate, did not appear until 2018.[79]

The stories in that document ranged from the supportive to the traumatic, and research of my own into the experience of women in Baptist ministry uncovered further stories of pain and difficulty. Although none of the questions specifically related to motherhood, respondents shared the following experiences: 'having young family made pastoral ministry difficult . . . for this reason I moved first to part-time ministry and then to sector ministry which combined more easily with family responsibilities'; 'I had to wait until my children were a certain age before I could imbark [sic] upon the demanding journey of studying alongside being a minister'; 'I had to put family before call'; 'when I fell pregnant...the church chose not to continue my placement long enough to complete my training after my baby was born'; and 'taking maternity leave has massively affected my

---

[78] Ruth Gouldbourne, 'Baptists, Women and Ministry', *Feminist Theology* 26.1 (2017): 62.

[79] See *Becoming a Mother in Ministry*, accessed at https://www.baptist.org.uk/Articles/536636/Becoming_a_mother.aspx. I was one of the small group of women who gathered to relate our experiences and draft the document. While the focus was on women becoming mothers while in ministry, it is worth remembering that others will have entered ministry already as mothers.

role and how I am now perceived.'[80] In a reflection that was both personal and theological, Baptist minister Katy Ruddle noted that she was asked on several occasions during the ministerial recognition process what she would do if she had children, while her husband did not face the same questions when going through the same process a short time later,[81] her suspicion being that 'the motivation behind the question of my childcare arrangements came from the assumption that ministry belongs in the public arena and is hence male,'[82] although she also acknowledged that in reality ministry and motherhood had not always been in conflict and there had in fact been considerable advantages to both her ministry and her daughter.[83]

Even without my own story, it would be clear to me that there are significant challenges as well as rich blessings when it comes to being a mother in Baptist ministry, and as such, there is a need for more open reflection and conversation. Women are still in the minority among Baptist ministers,[84] and not all of them are mothers, so it is perhaps not surprising that recognition of our experiences and adequate support for our situations has been

---

[80] Unpublished research conducted as part of my MA in Theology, Mission and Ministry in 2017.

[81] Katy Ruddle, 'Motherhood and Ministry: a lived response' in *Baptist Ministers' Journal* 293 (2006): 7.

[82] Ruddle, 'Motherhood and Ministry', 8.

[83] Ruddle, 'Motherhood and Ministry', 7.

[84] According to the Ignite report of 2015, 14% of Baptist ministers at that time were female. See 'Ignite: Final Report' accessed at https://www.baptist.org.uk/Publisher/File.aspx?ID=163522

slow, but that does not make it any less frustrating for those of us who still feel like pioneers long after we might have hoped that the last fragments of the stained-glass ceiling would have been swept away. We are not helped by the fact that the formal literature in this area is limited, which means that conversations about motherhood and ministry are normally restricted to the places where they are already coexisting,[85] with the result that motherhood does not feature prominently in broader conversations about how we understand and practice ministry. I hope that by putting some of my personal life into the public sphere, I might prompt reflection in places that have not yet seen a mother in ministry, as well as provide some moments of recognition and solidarity for those who have walked or will walk similar paths.

Personal Experiences of Motherhood and Ministry

The connection between my two vocations actually began before I was living in either of them. At the point at which I began seriously discerning a call to accredited ministry, I had been married for around a year and wanted to be open to the possibility of children, but I couldn't see how the two would fit together. My own mother stopped working when I was born, only returning to part-time work once my younger sister and I were both at school, and in the brief moments that I had thought about raising my own

---

[85] One thing that was clear from the gathering that led to *Becoming a Mother in Ministry* was that churches had not considered maternity leave until it was a live issue.

hypothetical children, I had assumed I would follow a similar pattern, but it seemed impossible to think that I could step back for five years or more to focus on family during my training or the early years of my ministry.[86] I didn't feel able to ask any of the questions I had around ministry and family life as part of the discernment process, but fortunately, I did speak of them with my mother, who sagely told me that she didn't believe God would ask me to sacrifice having children for ministry, but that I might have to sacrifice my expectations of what having children would look like. That gave me the confidence and peace I needed to trust that if ministry and motherhood were both right, then somehow, they would be right together.

I certainly needed that trust when I found out I was expecting my son a week into ministerial training. The minister I was working alongside must have laughed for a solid minute when I told him I was pregnant and then again for another minute when I said I wanted to take a short maternity leave and keep training. His laughter was not meant unkindly — I think it came more from shock than anything else, and he was unfailingly supportive from that point on — but it did mark the beginning of a gendered response to my pregnancy. The men involved in my training all emphasised that I could take more maternity leave if I needed it, while the women simply assured me that we would make it work. It left me with the distinct impression that the men thought I was

---

[86] While I did not receive this advice personally, 'it's not uncommon for women to be told not to get pregnant during training or first post', Middleton, *Breaking the Mould,* 55.

being ambitious or unrealistic, while the women knew it was possible because they had already done it. I know those men were speaking with the best of intentions, and I was grateful for their support, but I wonder now if they had not been sufficiently aware of the experiences of their female colleagues to know that others had already done what I was suggesting. That surely underscores the importance of this kind of storytelling, although if honesty is rightly to be privileged, then we must be prepared to hear stories that challenge as well as those that reassure.

Having welcomed my son and returned to ministry, I started to learn just how much I could achieve one-handed and with little sleep, although it would be fair to say that some days ran more smoothly than others. I recall that on one occasion, I stepped forward to preach and realised I had baby sick on my shoulder, and one morning, I was so tired from night feeding that I arrived at college ready to lead morning prayers with my top inside out. More recently, I had to dash out of a church meeting while members were in discussion groups in order to change my daughter's nappy before the smell hit everyone's nostrils. These incidents may seem improper to some, but I feel no shame in them as they simply reflect the truth that motherhood and ministry are interwoven strands of my life, and I cannot always keep one out of the other. 'This can be a cause of significant stress, and I understand that maintaining a greater distance or distinction is important at times and may be necessary for others, but where I find balance it more often looks like integration than separation. One of the most important lessons I learnt during my training was that God calls us as we are, and those of us who find ourselves in these roles must minister and mother out of our authentic natures, finding what works for us and our families and our churches.

I have now had two stints of maternity leave, and so I can conclusively say that I am terrible at it. I took my son to his first church event at ten days old, and it would have been sooner if it were not for a return trip to the hospital with jaundice. By the end of my three-month maternity leave, I had taken him to support the faith stand at a local community day and join an affirming Christian presence at Leeds Pride. There was a greater separation from church during my second maternity leave because of the coronavirus pandemic, but we were still at Zoom coffee after the online service every Sunday. I left my daughter for the first time to conduct a wedding on a keeping in touch day, and I took another day to write down the dreams and schemes which were rattling around my head during long sleepless nights and which came to form the basis of our future planning. I found it very hard to step away from ministry because I didn't know who I was or what I should do without it.[87] I am sufficiently self-aware that I can recognise that this was a time when motherhood and ministry should have been less integrated, and I did not find the right balance for that season. I doubt I am alone in this experience, however, and I suspect there are many more ministers who find days off and holidays similarly overshadowed by ministry

---

[87] For what it is worth, I actually err towards a functional view of accredited ministry, but I believe it is underpinned by the ontological call to ministry, which is experienced by all Christians, and sometimes it is hard to separate the two.

concerns. Neither motherhood nor ministry are easily laid down once they have been picked up, and perhaps those of us who happily muddle church and personal life together need better support to set the tasks of ministry aside when circumstances require, without risking existential crisis.

There are more stories I could relate and reflect on, but for the moment, I want to change direction. I commented earlier that the literature on motherhood and ministry is scarce. I think this is perfectly understandable, as these lived practices keep us busy enough without writing about them. The honest truth is that by the time the children are in bed, and my to-do list is settled, I have little brain space for anything but junk television, and if this piece makes it into print, it will be by the skin of my teeth and the grace of the editors. I do, however, wonder if there are also less practical and more ideological factors at play. Have we not reflected on or used the language of motherhood because we have seen ministry as male? And if we have seen ministry as male, is it because we have seen God as male? The very existence of myself and my sisters in ministry reveals the lie beneath the assumptions which drive the first question, and I have no wish to justify us or our ministry here. I will, however, give some space in the next section to challenging the assumptions behind the second question by briefly considering images of motherhood and God.

Motherhood and the Nature of God

There are a number of references we could pick up on here, from the ice emerging from God's womb (Job 38:9) to God pictured as a mother bear robbed of her cubs (Hosea 13:8), to Jesus picturing himself as a mother hen (Luke 13:34). Lauren Winner notes three images related to childbirth and childrearing which are used by Isaiah to characterise God — God is a labouring woman gasping and panting (Isaiah 42:14), a midwife promising to bring delivery (Isaiah 66:9), and a mother offering comfort to her child (Isaiah 66:13).[88] While scholars disagree on the authorship of Isaiah, Winner takes the view that these passages all come from Deutero-Isaiah, 'written while a significant slice of the Judean population was living in exile in Babylon . . . to assure the exiled people that God has not abandoned them.'[89] It is easy to see why images of new life and maternal care would speak powerfully into that situation, and it is somewhat frustrating to recognise that these metaphors are not better known today. There cannot have been a moment in history when God's people did not long to see God birth something new, and yet it is still considered radical to speak of God as Mother.

Winner focuses on the first of the three images, noting that while the lectionary draws from Isaiah at key moments in the Christian year, the prophet's description of God as a labouring woman does not feature once, so that 'if you attend a church that follows the lectionary, you will never hear that verse read on Sunday from the lectern.'[90] She wonders if 'the lectionary crafters find the picture

---

[88] Lauren Winner, *Wearing God: Clothing, Laughter, Fire, and Other Overlooked Ways of Meeting God* (New York: Harper Collins, 2015), 60.

[89] Winner, *Wearing God*, 60-1.

[90] Winner, *Wearing God*, 61.

of God squatting and grunting in labour as disconcerting as [she does].'[91] While the lectionary shies away from what it finds uncomfortable, disconcerting does not mean to be avoided for Winner, who finds these images utterly compelling 'precisely in their discomfiture' as they 'bespeak God's intimate bodily involvement with our redemption,'[92] and suggests that 'God will be identified with humanity, utterly.'[93]

Winner also finds the image of God in childbirth compelling because 'Isaiah is naming as the activity of God something readily available to most of the world's women.'[94] She remarks in parentheses that 'in our own cultural moment,' unprecedented numbers of women have not experienced labour while unprecedented numbers of men have witnessed it,[95] and it strikes me that this serves to remind us that until very recently, childbirth was an almost exclusively female space. We know little of the author of these verses, so what follows can only be prophetic imagination, but if it is unlikely that a male prophet had been near enough to childbirth to write so intimately about it, then perhaps these verses are the words of an unknown female prophet.[96] And if it is unlikely that a male audience would have witnessed labour

---

[91] Winner, *Wearing God*, 61.

[92] Winner, *Wearing God*, 60.

[93] Winner, *Wearing God*, 63.

[94] Winner, *Wearing God*, 60.

[95] Winner, *Wearing God*, 60.

[96] I believe I first heard this suggested in an episode of the 'Politics in the Pulpit?' podcast produced by the Joint Public Issues Team. The podcast can be accessed at https://jpit.uk/politicsinthepulpit.

at sufficiently close range to understand the metaphor, then perhaps these verses were written specifically with women in mind.

When I first considered those possibilities, I felt a shiver of excitement. Women are so often marginalised within the scriptures that there is something quite thrilling about the idea that in these verses, we hear their voices and sense their presence. But we ought not to forget what we have set out to do, as while these images use the language of motherhood to speak of God, providing a strong argument for it being a valid theological category, there is more work to be done if we are to use the language of motherhood to speak of ministry. There is also a danger that the interpretation I have suggested reserves mothering as a model or metaphor which is used by and resonates with women alone, but I want to ask if mothering can offer something more broadly, and so we must continue on.

Ministry as Motherhood, Motherhood as Ministry

Countless models and metaphors have been employed to speak of ministry, none claiming to be complete or definitive, but each offering something particular. Here we turn to consider how motherhood might provide language and imagery with which we might better understand and express ministry, for the benefit of those who minister but also for the benefit of those who are ministered to. Perhaps the person who has written most extensively on motherhood and ministry to date is Emma Percy.[97] In the final section of the work based on her doctoral research, she draws on the experience and language of mothering to name a number of aspects of ministry, skills which she believes 'often go unrecognised, unarticulated and thus unvalued.'[98] These are 'the art of cherishing,' 'the art of comforting,' 'embodied ways of knowing and communicating,' 'multitasking and multi-attending,' 'homemaking and housekeeping,' and "weaning and managing change.'[99] While I will not attempt to reflect on these skills here, I commend her insights and offer them as further reading if this is an area which has sparked interest.

What I do want to pick up on is Percy's contention that these skills are 'as much about attitudes and ways of being as they are about what is done,'[100] and that undervaluing them undermines ministry and 'make[s] it hard for clergy to recognise their own successes and take pleasure and joy in all that they do.'[101] My first observation is that this draws out the ontological aspects of both motherhood and ministry. Debates around functional and ontological views of ministry may be common in theological colleges but are perhaps not well understood among

---

[97] Percy's writing focuses on the role of an Anglican parish priest, which has its own peculiarities distinct from that of the Baptist minister, but most of her ideas carry across even if not all of the language does.

[98] Emma Percy, *Mothering as a Metaphor for Ministry* (Farnham: Ashgate, 2014), 135.

[99] Percy, *Mothering as a Metaphor*, 135-36.

[100] Percy, *Mothering as a Metaphor*, 135.

[101] Percy, *Mothering as a Metaphor*, 153.

congregations. If we follow Percy's lead in drawing from the lexicon of motherhood, however, we might suggest that there is a ministerial instinct in the same way there is a maternal instinct, expressing in more familiar language the idea that ministry is lived out of a person's very being. My second reflection is that it is not only ministers who need to place more value on the skills Percy names. Guilt at not having accomplished enough is real for many people, not least the mother who has spent the day staring at the pile of laundry to be folded while she is pinned to the sofa by a nursing baby, and ministers need to respond to this by affirming that who we are is as important as what we do. In this way, bringing insights from motherhood can not only refine our understanding of ministry but also offer encouragement to the wider church.

Underpinning the skills common to motherhood and ministry, Percy speaks of the need for attentive love. 'Just as mothers need to learn through trial and error how the actual child differs from the abstract child of the antenatal classes or the ones described in the childcare books, so clergy need to learn through practice about the real parish and people entrusted to their care.'[102] This means that 'parish clergy need to look, listen and absorb the community they are called to serve' in much the same way that a mother spends time 'simply sitting and looking at her child.'[103] I wonder if ministers spend the same proportion of time playing with their congregations as they do with their children, if they are as quick

---

[102] Percy, *Mothering as a Metaphor*, 107.
[103] Percy, *Mothering as a Metaphor*, 109.

to celebrate whatever the equivalent of full marks on a spelling test might be for their members, if they take as much time to sit with real or figurative grazed knees and bumped heads. I suspect the answer for many, if not most, is no, and so I wonder if perhaps ministers need to be encouraged to spend more time simply sitting and looking at their churches.

This will have its joys, but it will also have its struggles, and it certainly has its responsibilities. Percy points to 'parallels between the maternal demand to create and maintain the relationships and environments in which children themselves can develop towards maturity and the parish priest's role to create and maintain the Christian community of the local church in which and through which people are able to grow ever deeper in faith and understanding.'[104] The task of both mother and minister is to support the growth of those in their care, but power imbalances in those relationships can make it hard to do this without exercising inappropriate control, and so we must seek to ensure that a maternalistic approach does not take on the negative connotations of paternalism, and beware that mothering does not become smothering. Natalie Carnes writes powerfully about the difficulty mothers face in 'learning to become two,'[105] as the child they have carried takes on their own life and develops their own character and will. She relays a standoff between her and her young daughter, confessing her mixed motivations in demanding that the

---

[104] Percy, *Mothering as a Metaphor*, 103.

[105] Natalie Carnes, *Motherhood: A Confession*, (Stanford: Stanford University Press, 2020), 112.

girl apologise for accidentally hurting a friend, saying with searing honesty, 'I wanted you to flourish and be good. I wanted you to obey me and look like a good mother.'[106] Ministers similarly need to recognise these motives in themselves and seek to lean into the former, guiding and caring without infantilising or dominating, and seeking always the flourishing of the church, not the flattering of the ego.

Percy, therefore, contends that 'both [motherhood and ministry] need to think hard about questions of dependence, independence and interdependence,'[107] and here I think we might offer a distinctively Baptist perspective. In Percy's Anglican setting, 'people are dependent on a parish priest for aspects of ministry . . . she is the gatekeeper for certain rituals and sacraments,'[108] but that is not true within our Baptist tradition. Having grown up in the Church of England before finding my home and my feet in the Baptist denomination at the age of twenty, I was slightly taken aback when invited to preside at communion as a guest preacher before I had even been accepted for training, but it was a privilege to accept the invitation, and I am sure that it was a significant moment in the maturing of my faith and the discernment of my call. This lack of gatekeeping means there is greater potential for developing interdependency within our churches, and ministers should be proactive in making the most of it. Here again, drawing on motherhood may be constructive. The relationship between a

---

[106] Carnes, *Motherhood: A Confession*, 100.

[107] Percy, *What Clergy Do*, 65.

[108] Percy, *What Clergy Do*, 69.

mother and her child will change as the latter becomes more independent, and while this may feel disorientating as it happens, it is expected and, therefore, ultimately accepted. Understanding that ministers must go through a similar process with church members may help them prepare for the changing dynamics this will entail.

Percy also draws on the concept of being a 'good enough' mother, developed in the 1950s by paediatrician Donald Winnicott, to explore the possibility of being a 'good enough' priest.[109] She writes that to be a good enough mother is to be consistent in meeting a child's needs while allowing them to develop their own capacities,[110] the implication being that the good enough minister must do likewise for those in their care, although there is a danger that this too easily glides over the pain that arises when being 'good enough' simply isn't possible. Of course, each child and church member will have different needs and capacities, and so what it means to be good enough can only be worked out in context through attentive love. It is common for new mothers to be told not to bother reading parenting books because the baby won't have read them, and perhaps we might say the same to new ministers whose congregations are unlikely to be well-versed in the wealth of literature on church leadership. There is surely much wisdom to be found in the pages of these texts, and there is certainly value in the sharing of stories that happens through parental groups and ministerial clusters, but ultimately, both

---

[109] Percy, *What Clergy Do*, 27ff.
[110] Percy, *What Clergy Do*, 28.

motherhood and ministry are arts, not sciences, and so 'developing the ability to be good enough in either ministry or mothering means developing virtues rather than following rules.'[111]

We have acknowledged tensions within motherhood and ministry, but for those of us who exercise both vocations, there can also be tension between them. It is a trivial and slightly comical example, but when we applied for my son to attend the local church school, I had to sign one form as his mum and another as his minister, with a note explaining why it was the same signature on both. If I am in some ways mother to my congregation,[112] I am also minister to my children, and it is not always easy to be both at once. Amy Stertz echoes something of my own experience when she writes 'I wrestle with doubt, stress, and feelings of inadequacy both at home and at work . . . As I try to honour one calling, I neglect the other . . . I want very much to be the one who guides my daughter through worship . . . But I am equally called to the platform and desire to help my congregation encounter God.'[113] There is a sense of loss here, but there is also an opportunity to expand our

---

[111] Percy, *What Clergy Do*, 34.

[112] Even after extensive reflection on the similarities between motherhood and ministry, it still feels strange to write that in such stark terms, especially as I am at least two decades younger than most of my congregation. I'm not yet sure where to take that response, but I do want to note it.

[113] Amy R Stertz, 'Mom or Minister?' in *A Divine Duet: Ministry and Motherhood* (Macon: Smyth and Helwys, 2013), 102-103. Stertz also speaks very positively of her dual calling, saying that each has made her better at the other. See Stertz. 'Mom or Minister?', 101.

understanding of both motherhood and ministry. Ministry is not just the work of accredited ministers but is the collective life and witness of the church, and this is perhaps especially true for Baptists, with our foundational belief in the ministry of all believers. At the same time, church communities can provide wonderful examples of allomothering, the care of children by someone other than their natural mother. If I am not guiding my children through worship or wiping their noses and helping them build impossible towers in the Prayground,[114] then I can be sure that someone else will be, and there is rich blessing for everyone in that.

A final point may further expand our view beyond the experience of the individual mother or minister, as we might consider motherhood as an image for the church itself and the ministry we all share in. Carnes ends her reflection on motherhood with a striking image of the church as a mother: 'With all creation, the Mother-Church groans in her birth-pains, waiting for the arrival of Christ that will end her labour . . . Imitating and sustained by Your own motherhood, she labours on, anticipating in hope the eternal rest of new creation crowning.'[115] The church must show

---

[114] This is the name we have given to what was previously the children's corner, a space where children can play but also engage with prayer and scripture on their own terms, although my son is adamant that adults are welcome too. The idea came from Margaret Pritchard Houston's suggestion of a Pray and Play corner, for which see Margaret Pritchard Houston, *Beyond the Children's Corner: Creating a Culture of Welcome for All Ages* (London: Church House, 2020), 56ff.

[115] Percy, *What Clergy Do*, 181.

the same attentive love to the world as mothers show to their children and ministers show to their congregations, and the same skills of cherishing and comforting and communicating and multitasking and homemaking and managing change must be honed and employed as we 'bear personal witness [and] take part in the evangelisation of the world.'[116]

Concluding Thoughts

There is much else that might be explored here, and I hope others will pick up the threads I have left loose. In her exploration of Isaiah, Winner introduced the image of God as midwife as well as mother, and I think there is much potential for developing midwifery as a metaphor for ministry.[117] I am interested too in Percy's idea of the priest as housekeeper, with the attendant questions of what it means to create and maintain a spiritual

---

[116] The third article of the Declaration of Principle of the Baptist Union of Great Britain says, 'That it is the duty of every disciple to bear personal witness to the Gospel of Jesus Christ, and to take part in the evangelisation of the world.'

[117] For example, John Colwell suggests that 'the analogy [between midwife and minister] effectively draws attention to the instrumental and mediatorial nature of nature of Christian ministry' as both assist in the process of new life without themselves creating it. He suggests that 'like all analogies, it ultimately fails' as midwifery is an acquired skill whereas ministry is a gift of God, although it could be countered that a midwife must possess inherent gifts and a minster must be able to develop new skills, and so the analogy is stronger than Colwell suggests. See John Colwell, *Promise and Presence: An Exploration in Sacramental Theology* (Milton Keynes: Paternoster, 2005), 216.

home.[118] I have also given only passing thought to the difficulties and limitations of motherhood as a model and metaphor for ministry, but we must recognise that the language and images employed here may be unhelpful for a number of reasons. Motherhood can evoke complicated feelings for many, and we should avoid any assumption or expectation that it is synonymous with womanhood, so while I think there is much here that could enrich ministerial training, in contexts where it is not possible to simply skip past material that may be uncomfortable, the language of motherhood should always be offered with pastoral sensitivity, and with the expectation that it is only taken up where it offers comfort or clarity.

On a very pragmatic note, I want to suggest that greater support is needed in order that those who are called to both motherhood and ministry might flourish and offer the fullness of their gift to the church and to their children. We have already heard some of the practical and logistical difficulties of balancing motherhood and ministry, which need to be properly accounted for within our church structures, so that no woman is left to lament that 'my two greatest passions have provided an abundant life . . . I just wish I could have lived them simultaneously,'[119] but there are emotional strains too. Allison-Glenny has written powerfully about her own

---

[118] Percy, *What Clergy Do*, 128.

[119] Natalie Nicholas Adams, 'A Tale of Two Callings' in *A Divine Duet,* 8. Natalie served in Baptist churches in Georgia and North Carolina, rather than in our own union, but I would be shocked if her story was not repeated here many times over.

experience of perinatal mental illness in ministry and the need for theological reflection which is able to deal in the unsafe and the unresolved.[120] '[Renita] Weems concludes that the spirituality of a working mother cannot be the same as it was before motherhood,'[121] and '[Bonnie Miller-McLemore] is clear that pregnancy, childbirth, and breastfeeding affect the ways that she understands sacrifice and selfishness.'[122] Ministers who become mothers therefore need pastoral support to navigate these existential changes.

Returning to our earlier observation that motherhood is not monolithic, it is vital that we continue to listen to a wide range of experiences. Womanist theologian Monica Coleman offers the insight that 'working motherhood has signified something different for Black women than it has for White women,' in part because 'there have long been informal community mothers and other-mothers in African American communities' and in part because 'the structure of United States slavery and racism resulted in the fact that Black motherhood and the work of Black women have long been intertwined.'[123] While Coleman speaks out of a specifically North American context, her work is a powerful reminder that intersecting identities such as race and class will

---

[120] Elizabeth Allison-Glenny, 'The disembodiment of birthing and the incapacity to theologically reflect: a perspective from perinatal mental illness in ministry', *Practical Theology* 16:3 (2023): 330-40.

[121] Monica A Coleman, 'Sacrifice, Surrogacy and Salvation', *Black Theology* 12:3 (2014): 207.

[122] Coleman, 'Sacrifice, Surrogacy and Salvation', 209.

[123] Coleman, 'Sacrifice, Surrogacy and Salvation', 201.

shape the lived experience of motherhood. It is important to acknowledge that there will be stories to be heard about fatherhood and parenthood through adoption too, as well as the difficulties of balancing caring responsibilities for partners and parents. I cannot speak for those experiences because they are not my own, but I believe we would all be further enriched by them.

As I conclude, I wish to echo Alicia Davis Porterfield's prayer that 'we will begin intentionally incorporating these sacred stories of ministry and motherhood into our larger church life.'[124] I believe there is much to be gained from seeing motherhood as a metaphor and model for ministry, most particularly in the way it draws attention and gives value to more personal and relational aspects. I trust that every minister would recognise these as important if asked, but it is easy for them to be crowded out of ministry by observable tasks and measurable goals in a way that is less likely to happen in motherhood, and so the comparison may help redress the balance, leading us to 'a fuller vision of incarnational ministry.'[125] I also believe that the sacred stories of motherhood offer insights for the church beyond the realm of ministry. Coleman draws on Miller-McLemore's claim that 'mother love may be among the greatest sources of spiritual and moral insight' to suggest that 'motherhood changes the kinds of theological questions that we ask,'[126] and Delores Williams has brought womanist theologies of motherhood to bear on theories

---

[124] Alicia Davis Porterfield, 'Introduction' in *A Divine Duet*, 2.

[125] Kristin Adkins Whitesides 'That's Life!' in *A Divine Duet,* 124.

[126] Coleman, 'Sacrifice, Surrogacy and Salvation', 202.

of the atonement, demanding that Black women have sacrificed too much for sacrifice to ever be salvific, so that for her it is not the cross that saves but the new vision for humankind given by Jesus through his life and ministry.[127] There is profound wisdom and challenging thought here - if we are willing to hear it.

It is my hope that some of what has been shared will help ministers to develop the mothering aspects of their own ministry, whether they are mothers themselves or not, but also that it will help mothers to recognise their responsibilities as ministers, whether they exercise a formal ministry or not. I hope, too, that this act of storytelling and reflection points to something beyond either motherhood or ministry. The Catholic writer Margaret Hebblethwaite reflected that 'we must listen to God in the experience of our own motherhood; then perhaps we will be able to share something with the community that no one else can bring,'[128] but motherhood could be replaced in that sentence by any lived experience, and so I am delighted that this piece will sit alongside others reflecting on different identities. May we all listen to God in the experiences of our own lives so that we may share what no one else can.

---

[127] Coleman, 'Sacrifice, Surrogacy and Salvation', 203.

[128] Margaret Hebblethwaite, *Motherhood and God* (London: Bloomsbury, 1994), 119.

4   The Intersection of Baptists and Disability

Martin Hobgen

Mark Medley suggests that tradition 'provides a communal space in which people can dwell and a set of practices that shapes how participants live a way of life.'[129] The experience of many disabled people is that of exclusion from such communal space or being passive observers rather than active participants.

This chapter will examine how disabled people were isolated from society and church from the early eighteenth to the late twentieth centuries. The significant change from a medical to a social understanding of disability in the late twentieth century is identified. This change, however, left relationships between disabled and non-disabled people in general terms. Drawing on Paul Fiddes' pastoral doctrine of the Trinity and Baptist understandings of covenant community, this chapter argues that covenant friendships are a significant way to foster the participatory inclusion of disabled people in Baptist church communities.

Intersectionality and Disability

---

[129] Mark S Medley, 'Stewards, Interrogators, and Inventors: Toward a Practice of Tradition', *Pro Ecclesia* 18.1 (2009): 80.

83

While this book explores Baptist intersectionality, disability is also intersectional, as is my experience of both. I write not only from the perspective of being a disabled person but as a white English male, ordained Baptist Minister, a wheelchair user, brought up in a lower-middle class family context, who is well educated, experienced various forms of employment, married but without children. My perspective would be significantly altered if any of these intersectionalities were different.

My experience of being disabled is itself shaped by a number of intersectionalities, those identified above and the fact that I have a medical condition, Spina Bifida, which created a congenital impairment, resulting in me being a full-time wheelchair user from the age of eight. Although I am paralysed from the waist down, the use of my arms and intellect are unaffected. My experiences of disability are, therefore, shaped by these embodied constraints rather than intellectual or other hidden disabilities.

Disabled People as Isolated Individuals

Prior to the industrial revolution, disabled people lived with their families, neighbours and friends in local communities which were predominantly rural.[130] During the eighteenth century, rapid industrialisation, alongside medicalisation and

---

[130] Phase one of Dan Finkelstein's three phase scheme. Vic Finkelstein, 'Disability and the Helper/Helped Relationship. An Historical View' in *Handicap in a Social World: A Reader* edited by Ann Brechin, Penny Liddiard, and John Swain (London: Open, University, 1981), 59-60.

institutionalisation, meant that disabled people were increasingly isolated from society and disability was understood to arise from the individual in terms of their medical condition.[131] This approach dominated the understanding of disability until the late twentieth century.

This understanding of disability and disabled people has come to be known as the Medical Model of Disability, sometimes referred to as the Individual/Medical Model of Disability (IMMD). In 1976, the World Health Organisation produced the following definitions that describe the Individual/Medical Model of Disability:

> *Impairment* – Any loss or abnormality of psychological, physiological or anatomical structure or function.
> *Disability* – Any restriction or lack (resulting from an impairment) of ability to perform an activity in the manner or within the range considered normal for a human being.
> *Handicap* – A disadvantage for an individual, resulting from an impairment or disability, that limits or prevents the fulfilment of a role (depending on age, sex, social and cultural factors) for that individual.[132]

---

[131] Phase two of Finkelstein's approach, 'Disability and the Helper/Helped Relationship', 60-63.

[132] Colin Barnes and G. Mercer, *Exploring Disability: A Sociological Introduction* (Wiley, 2010), 20. Quoting from WHO, *International Classification of Impairments, Disabilities, and Handicaps: A Manual of Classification Relating to the Consequences of Disease; Publ. For Trial Purposes in Accordance with Resolution Wha29.35 for the Twenty-Ninth*

This set of definitions was intended to address 'loss or abnormality' due to impairments. These impairments are measured by a medical diagnosis concerning 'psychological, physiological or anatomical structures or function'. Disability is defined as directly resulting from impairment and is seen in terms of inability to perform various activities. The problematic term 'handicap' then defines any disadvantage that a disabled person experiences as being due to the inability to fulfil a role that society assumes to be normal for a human being. It is this explicit focus on the individual and their impairment, from which disability and handicap are assumed to arise, which led to the naming of this set of definitions as the Individual/Medical Model of Disability.[133]

This understanding of disability has implications for the role of disabled people in society in general. The so-called 'problem of disability' is located with individuals and their impairments. The medical profession held power over disabled people, their treatment, and their lives in an asymmetric relationship. Disabled people were often institutionalised in workhouses and other institutions, subsequently becoming the objects of charitable giving.[134] The move from living among family, neighbours and

---

World Health Assembly, May 1976 (Geneva: World Health Organization, 1980), 27-29.

[133] Deborah Beth Creamer, *Disability and Christian Theology: Embodied Limits and Constructive Possibilities* (Oxford University Press, 2009), 22-25 outlines and critiques the Individual/Medical Model of Disability.

[134] Hannah Lewis, *Deaf Liberation Theology* (Aldershot: Ashgate, 2007), 85ff.

friends led to the isolation of disabled people from non-disabled people. There is evidence that disabled people still experience more loneliness and lack of friendships than non-disabled people, not least due to the attitudes of non-disabled people. The report, *'Someone cares if I'm not there'*,[135] by the charity Sense,[136] bluntly observes:

> Shockingly, one in two non-disabled people (49 per cent) don't believe they have anything in common with disabled people, and a quarter (26 per cent) admit they have avoided engaging in conversation with a disabled person.[137]

The intersectional nature of the experience of disability during this period has been largely overlooked until very recently. There was a wide range of other issues which informed the understanding of disability during this time; issues such as gender, class and race intersect with disability in ways that can both exacerbate and ameliorate the relationship between disabled and

---

[135] Sense, 'Someone Cares If I'm Not There' (2017), https://www.sense.org.uk/loneliness.

[136] 'Sense is a national charity that supports and campaigns for children and adults who have sensory impairments and complex needs. We provide tailored support, advice and information to individuals, their families, carers and the professionals who work with them,' *A Right to Friendship? Challenging the Barriers to Friendship for People with Disabilities* (2015); 'Someone Cares If I'm Not There', 40.

[137] 'Someone Cares If I'm Not There', 3.

non-disabled people.[138] Unlike race, class and gender, the 'solution' has historically been to rehabilitate disabled people so that they are 'normalised', enabling them to fit in and to live within mainstream, non-disabled society.[139]

This approach has subsequently shaped the church's understanding of disability and the relationship with disabled people in ways that have hindered inclusion. During this period, churches became significant providers of care and support to various groups, sometimes through the provision of institutional care. The institutional context of disabled people led to highly asymmetric relationships between disabled residents and non-disabled staff, perceived as 'helped' and 'helper.'[140] Nancy Eiesland has identified a number of ways that the IMMD has resulted in the exclusion of disabled people from churches: associating disability with sin or virtuous suffering; assuming disabled people are in need of charity; problematic readings of healing miracles; the unintentional and intentional exclusion of disabled people, physically, socially and theologically; and the silencing and ignoring of the voices of disabled people.[141]

---

[138] David M. Turner, *Disability in Eighteenth-Century England: Imagining Physical Impairment* (London: Routledge, 2012), 103-4, 22-4.

[139] See Anne Borsay, 'Disciplining Disabled Bodies: The Development of Orthopaedic Medicine in Britain, C.1800-1938' in *Social Histories of Disability and Deformity* edited by David M. Turner and Kevin Stagg (London: Routledge, 2006), 97.

[140] Finkelstein, 'Disability and the Helper/Helped Relationship.'

[141] Nancy L. Eiesland, *The Disabled God: Towards a Liberatory Theology of Disability* (Nashville: Abingdon, 1994), 53-7, 75-87, 94-98; John Swinton,

Recent research has shown how the IMMD has led to an impoverished pastoral care model of disability, which views disabled people as passive recipients.[142] Naomi Jacobs argues that the misuse of pastoral power has been the key to churches' pastoral care of disabled people, which has often been expressed in terms of charity. One result of this is that 'most theology of disability remains rooted in pastoral theology.'[143] I strongly suggest that the problem is not that theologies of disability are rooted in pastoral theology itself but that inappropriate 'pastoral care models' of disability are rooted in narrow and impoverished parodies of pastoral theology.[144] These parodies sustain problematic assumptions about disability's link to sin, requiring forgiveness, and to illness, requiring healing. She argues, correctly, I think, that such a skewed approach, in both pastoral care and theology, leads to the 'othering' of disabled people. This reinforces the 'doing for' relationship between disabled and non-

---

'Who Is the God We Worship? Theologies of Disability; Challenges and New Possibilities', *International Journal of Practical Theology* 14.2 (2011): 282.

[142] Naomi Lawson Jacobs, *The Upside-Down Kingdom of God: A Disability Studies Perspective on Disabled People's Experiences in Churches and Theologies of Disability* (SOAS University of London, 2019), 102f. See also Naomi Lawson Jacobs and Emily Richardson, *At the Gates: Disability, Justice and the Churches* (London: DLT, 2022).

[143] Jacobs, *The Upside-Down Kingdom of God*, 85.

[144] A valid critique of pastoral care is that it has failed to give proper attention to disability, although the situation has changed in recent years. Jacobs seems at times to equate pastoral care and pastoral theology, Jacobs, *The Upside-Down Kingdom of God*, 86. She also uses the terms 'pastoral care model' and 'pastoral model' interchangeably.

disabled people, which denies disabled people agency, silences their voices, and can lead to segregated patterns of ministry.[145]

Disabled People in non-Disabled Society

There has been a very significant change in the understanding of disability during the last three decades of the twentieth century.[146] This has a profound effect on relationships between disabled people and a society dominated by non-disabled people. Disability activists and disabled academics developed the Social Model of Disability (SMD) in the 1970s and 1980s. It is rooted within what was at that time, the newly emerging field of disability sociology, together with a growing disability rights movement. From these arose a two-stage definition of impairment and disability:

> *Impairment* – Lacking part or all of a limb, or having a defective limb, organ or mechanism in the body.
> *Disability* – The disadvantage or restriction of activity caused by a contemporary social organisation which takes no or little account of people who have a physical impairment and thus excludes them from participation in the mainstream of social activities.[147]

---

[145] Jacobs, *The Upside-Down Kingdom of God*, 85-8.

[146] Phase three of Finkelstein's approach, Finkelstein, 'Disability and the Helper/Helped Relationship', 63.

[147] Barnes and Mercer, 20. Quoting from WHO, 27-29.

Disability has been described by the Union of the Physically Impaired Against Segregation (UPIAS), in the following way:

> It is society which disables physically impaired people. Disability is something imposed on top of our impairments, by the way we are unnecessarily isolated and excluded from full participation in society. Disabled people are therefore an oppressed group.[148]

The Social Model was deliberately intended to break the link between the individual who lives with some level of impairment and their experience of disability, which is the result of the attitudes and actions towards them by other people, groups, organisations, and society. Rather than expecting disabled people to change, be cured, or be healed in order to be included in all aspects of society, this model emphasises the need for social attitudes towards people living with impairments to change. This results in actions being taken by society that enable disabled people to be included.[149] These necessary actions range from physical access, for example, the provision of physical aids such as wheelchairs and hearing aids, to the social, political, and economic changes required for disabled people to actively

---

[148] Tom Shakespeare, *Disability Rights and Wrongs Revisited* (London: Routledge, 2013), 12 quoting UPIAS, *Fundamental Principles of Disability: Being a Summary of the Discussion Held on 22nd November, 1975 and Containing Commentaries from Each Organisation* (London: Union of the Physically Impaired Against Segregation, Disability Alliance, 1976), 3.

[149] Dan Goodley, *Disability Studies: An Interdisciplinary Introduction* (1st ed.; London: SAGE, 2010), 27-31.

participate rather than passively observe. This emerges from a separation of the assumed link between impairment and disability.

For churches, this model moves the focus to emphasise the importance of relationships between church communities and disabled people within and beyond the local church. This has resulted in a significant improvement in the physical access and facilities of many churches. By focusing so much on attitudes and barrier removal, however, it has done little to facilitate the development of inclusive and empowering relationships between disabled and non-disabled people. These relationships remain at a general level, between two distinct groups of 'the disabled' and 'the able-bodied,'[150] with a lack of mutual inter-personal relationships between them.

It is important to note that although writers in the USA often use the term 'Social Model of Disability,' there are many occasions when the model that is being used is properly called the Minority Group Model of Disability (MGMD). Within this model, Disabled people are understood to be:

> a group of people, who because of their physical or cultural characteristics, are singled out from the others in the society in which they live for differential and unequal

---

[150] 'Able-bodied' is used here, rather than 'non-disabled', to emphasise the othering of disabled people in this approach.

treatment, and who therefore regard themselves as objects of collective discrimination.[151]

This approach has achieved significant improvements in the inclusion of disabled people in the US.[152] Its major weakness, however, is the necessary maintenance of two distinct groups, 'the disabled' and 'the able bodied'. This restricts the potential for truly mutual and inclusive relationships between disabled and non-disabled people. The nature of disability has been discussed within various aspects of theology for many years,[153] but it was the publication of Nancy Eiesland's *The Disabled God* in 1994 that marked the emergence of a coherent body of theological exploration described as Theology of Disability or Disability Theology.[154]

Disability Theology has made some positive attempts to improve the inclusion of disabled people in church communities.[155] In

---

[151] Eiesland, *The Disabled God*, 63.

[152] Such as the Americans with Disabilities Act (1990).

[153] For a thorough exploration of the biblical narrative's portrayal of disability and disabled people see Sarah J Melcher, Mikeal Carl Parsons, and Amos Yong, *The Bible and Disability: A Commentary* (Waco, TX: Baylor University Press, 2017) and Brian Brock and John Swinton (eds.), *Disability in the Christian Tradition: A Reader* (Grand Rapids, MI: Eerdmans, 2012).

[154] The work of Stanley Hauerwas and Jean Vanier concerning people with learning disabilities preceded this by a couple of decades.

[155] Some key texts published since Eiesland's *The Disabled God* include Kathy Black, *A Healing Homiletic: Preaching and Disability* (Nashville, TN: Abingdon, 1996); Jennie Weiss Block, *Copious Hosting: A Theology of Access for People with Disabilities* (New York: Continuum, 2002); and Thomas E.

particular, it has challenged the erroneous link between disability and sin, requiring forgiveness, and the assumption that disabled people need to be physically healed before they can participate in church communities. Few of the writers, however, pay serious attention to inter-personal relationships between disabled and non-disabled people. Of those that consider this the relationship is left in general terms. A few mention friendships but leave the nature of the relationship undeveloped.

Trinity and Covenant Communities

The change in our understanding of disability from characteristics of individuals to the relationships between people suggests we consider the importance of our relationship with the Trinitarian God and the nature of our covenant relationships with God and one another.

Paul Fiddes, in his book *Participating in God*, explores the pastoral implications of a particular perspective on the relational Trinity.[156] Two aspects of his work are particularly helpful in

---

Reynolds, *Vulnerable Communion: A Theology of Disability and Hospitality* (Grand Rapids, MI: Brazos, 2008).

[156] For a succinct summary of the relationship between Fiddes' approach and the vast scope of Trinitarian doctrines see Daniel John Sutcliffe-Pratt, *Covenant and Church for Rough Sleepers: A Baptist Ecclesiology in Conversation with the Trinitarian Pastoral Theology of Paul S. Fiddes* (Oxford: Regent's Park College, 2017), 7-14. For a dialogue between theologians who hold different positions on the doctrine of the Trinity see Jason S. Sexton (ed.), *Two Views on the Doctrine of the Trinity* (Grand Rapids:

94

developing an understanding of covenant communities that enable the participatory inclusion of disabled people. Firstly, the concept of 'persons as relations' and secondly, the importance of 'participation' in the life of God and God's covenantal relationship with all of creation.

The first key characteristic of Fiddes' understanding of God as Trinity concerns relationality, especially between its 'persons'. He writes: 'It is not human individual persons but relations between them, in all their diversity and depth, that offers a helpful analogy to what we call divine "person."' [157] Fiddes proposes a shift of emphasis from 'persons *in* relation' to 'persons *as* relation,' which enables him to prioritise the centrality of relationships. [158] If we speak not simply about an analogy between God and human beings but also in terms of relationships, new possibilities begin to take shape. [159] The models of a Social Trinity and a Relational Trinity are, at the root, both relational. A clear focus on the nature of the relations, however, is particularly

Zondervan, 2014).

[157] Paul S. Fiddes, 'Relational Trinity: Radical Perspective' in *Two Views on the Doctrine of the Trinity*, 105.

[158] Colin E. Gunton, *The One, the Three, and the Many: God, Creation and the Culture of Modernity* (Cambridge: Cambridge University Press, 1993); Paul S. Fiddes, *Participating in God: A Pastoral Doctrine of the Trinity* (Westminster John Knox Press, 2000); Stephen R. Holmes, *The Quest for the Trinity: The Doctrine of God in Scripture, History, and Modernity* (IVP, 2012) all discuss issues of what form of divine/creation analogy is appropriate.

[159] The nature of personhood and embodiment can never be completely removed from any discussion of the nature of disability and the inclusion of disabled people.

helpful when it comes to focusing on relationships between disabled and non-disabled people.

The other key characteristic of Fiddes' approach is the concept of 'participation.' He writes:

> the point of Trinitarian language is not to provide an example to copy, but to draw us into participation in God, out of which human life can be transformed. But the language of Trinity certainly encourages the values of relationship, community and mutuality between persons. It is about interdependence and not domination.[160]

Fiddes puts clear water between his own understanding of God as Trinity and existing models of a Social Trinity. His use of the term *perichoresis* is especially significant.[161] The idea of *perichoresis* has been one of the ways, according to Sutcliffe-Pratt, that theologians explore a 'relationship between God-in-eternity and God-in-salvation.'[162] It is an important tool for exploring how 'three-ness' actually works in the concept of a triune God.[163] In a much-quoted definition, Catherine LaCugna writes:

---

[160] Fiddes, *Participating in God*, 66.

[161] Fiddes, *Participating in God*, 71-72.

[162] Sutcliffe-Pratt, *Covenant and Rough Sleepers*, 8.

[163] David S. Cunningham, 'Wellspring: Trinitarian Virtues' in *These Three Are One: The Practice of Trinitarian Theology* (Oxford: Blackwell, 1998), 180.

Perichoresis means being-in-one-another, permeation without confusion. No person exists by him/herself or is referred to him/herself; this would produce number and therefore division within God. Rather, to be a divine person is to be by nature in relation to other persons.[164]

This is certainly what those using the phrase 'persons *in* relationship' suggest, and the term has been used by proponents of a Social Trinity.[165] Fiddes' use of 'persons *as* relation' and 'participation in God' take the Social Trinity approach a stage further.[166]

The shift from 'persons *in* relationship' to 'persons *as* relation' enables us to leave behind any concerns about the personhood of disabled people, and to focus on the relations they have with other people. Fiddes is able to clarify this further using the metaphor of dance. When we think about dance, there is a tendency to focus on the dancers. When it comes to the 'divine dance,' Fiddes suggests that the focus shifts to 'perichoretic *movements* in human life, not with the *movers*.'[167] This is helpful when considering the

---

[164] Sutcliffe-Pratt, *Covenant and Rough Sleepers*, 9 quoting Catherine Mowry LaCugna, *God for Us: The Trinity and Christian Life* (HarperCollins, 1993).

[165] Moltmann, Boff, Cunningham are cited by Sutcliffe-Pratt, *Covenant and Rough Sleepers*, 9-11.

[166] Although LaCugna, *God for Us*, 243-44. uses the phrase 'persons as relation' she takes this to mean persons being constituted by relationships with other persons.

[167] Fiddes, *Participating in God*, 72. Italics original.

participatory inclusion of disabled people because the focus shifts to their dynamic relationships with non-disabled people and participation in the divine life.

Fiddes uses the metaphor of a dance to highlight the broad differences between Eastern and Western ways of speaking about God as Trinity. The Eastern tradition emphasises a dynamic relationality between the Father, Son and Holy Spirit. This lends itself to an image of an open 'progressive dance', in which God reaches out and draws us all into the relations within God's trinitarian life. The Western approach is more like a closed 'circle dance' among equal participants. This distinction is clearly promising as a way into understanding the participatory inclusion of disabled people.

The Western tradition takes us part of the way: emphasising some elements of participation, equality, and reciprocity. If, however, we stay with the image of a 'circle dance', we quickly see that this could introduce problems for our inclusion of people with disabilities. Circle dancers face inwards, with a strong impetus to maintain the integrity of the circle at all costs. If we think of a church community as an inward-facing circle, it would be relatively easy to exclude disabled people and others on the margins from participation in such a dance. If, instead, the dance is a 'progressive dance' into which others are invited, then it becomes possible to imagine the life of the church as open to the inclusion of those on the margins.[168]

---

[168] Andy Goodliff shows that Paul Fiddes and Brian Haymes argue for an

Today's Baptists have their roots back in the early seventeenth century. For early Baptists, intentional and mutual covenant-making formed a basis for the way they understood their relationships with God and fellow believers within and between particular local congregations.[169] The Baptists' intentional rejection of the authority of the State Church and recognition of the importance of the 'gathered church' was a hallmark of early Baptist life. Mutual relationships with one another before God were key to the local gathered congregation. This was strengthened during the seventeenth century by the emergence of the much-used metaphorical phrases, 'walking together' and 'watching over one another.'[170] These phrases made clear what it meant in practice to be a covenant community.[171] The dynamic images conveyed by these phrases suggest a group of people journeying together and a people open to the future. This is

---

open understanding of covenant relationships, while Roger Hayden and others argue for a more restrictive view. Andy Goodliff, *Renewing a Modern Denomination: A Study of Baptist Institutional Life in the 1990s* (Eugene, Oregon: Pickwick, 2021).

[169] The concept of covenant, a central theme to both the Old and New Testaments, influenced Baptist understandings of covenant relationships within and between congregations, see Paul S. Fiddes, *Tracks and Traces: Baptist Identity in Church and Theology* (Milton Keynes: Paternoster, 2003), 74-8.

[170] The metaphors used here, of 'walking' and 'watching', do not exclude those who cannot physically walk or who are blind or partially sighted, unless taken literally.

[171] Fiddes, *Tracks and Traces*, 22-3; Stephen R. Holmes, *Baptist Theology* (London: Continuum, 2012), 157.

emphasised by a third phrase which completes the picture: 'in ways known and to be made known.'[172] The Baptist church was not a group of individuals who simply happened to be 'walking together' in the same direction, but a group of believers who were intentionally 'walking together' with common purpose, caring for and supporting one another on the journey, as a group of friends might. The purpose and direction of the journey, they claimed, was not of their own choosing but was 'in the Lord's ways,'[173] which they discerned together in a church meeting.[174] When Baptists met as church, they did so intentionally, gathering together to seek 'the Lord's way.' In this way, mutual covenant relationships became strengthened within and between congregations.[175]

---

[172] Fiddes, *Tracks and Traces*, 22. discusses the importance of 'in ways to be made known', referred to as the 'further light clause.' See also Anthony R. Cross, '"Through a Glass Darkly": The Further Light Clause in Baptist Thought' in *Questions of Identity: Studies in Honour of Brian Haymes*, edited by Anthony R. Cross and Ruth M. B. Gouldbourne (Oxford: Regent's Park College, 2011).

[173] Fiddes, *Tracks and Traces*, 22. identifies this in the covenant of the separatist congregation at Gainsborough in 1606 or 1607.

[174] The 'church meeting' is commonly used as a noun, however deeper meaning may be revealed by using it as a verb, particularly in light of the first clause of the Declaration of Principle 'that each Church has the liberty, under the guidance of the Holy Spirit, to interpret and administer His Laws.' Richard Kidd (ed.), *Something to Declare: A Study of the Declaration of Principle*, 10.

[175] Lina Toth, 'From the Love of Friends to the Love of Strangers: Reflections on Friendship and Discipleship', *Baptistic Theologies* 7.2 (2015): 82-3 acknowledges the tension between personal convictions as we discern 'the rule of Christ' with others.

The late twentieth century saw renewed interest in the idea of 'covenant' and the broader implications both within and beyond Baptist church communities.[176] Fiddes was one of the key voices in the debates that took place during that period within and among Baptist churches, Associations, the Baptist Union and in wider Baptist and ecumenical conversations. Andy Goodliff, however, notes that despite Fiddes' influence, 'a theology of a union as covenant failed to embed itself in the language and practice of the Union.'[177] Despite this, Fiddes' understanding of God as Trinity, especially his use of 'persons *as* relation' and 'participation', enhances a Baptist covenant ecclesiology that enables the fostering of inclusive relationships.

An emphasis on God's desire for us to be drawn into the dance as participants and God's initiative in making covenant with all people, is fundamental for the way participation is expressed in covenant communities. Such an emphasis is not unique to Fiddes' approach to God as Trinity, but his emphasis on 'persons *as* relation' offers far-reaching implications for all relationships: in God, with God and with each other. All the social, economic, and other barriers that exist between people are potentially broken

---

[176] Darrell Jackson, *The Discourse of 'Belonging' and Baptist Church Membership in Contemporary Britain: Historical, Theological and Demotic Elements of a Post-Foundational Theological Proposal* (University of Birmingham, 2009), 68-71 examines the lack of attention to covenant during the twentieth century until the 1980s.

[177] Goodliff, *Renewing a Modern Denomination*, 125.

down.[178] Barriers of this kind were identified long ago in New Testament letters to churches in Galatia and Colossae, to which we can now add barriers between disabled and non-disabled people. Within this community, there is 'neither Jew nor Greek, slave nor free, male nor female . . . black nor white, able bodied, and handicapped [*sic*].'[179] If our relationships with other people could be modelled on our potential for relationship with God, then the non-discriminatory characteristics of God's covenant initiative could impact us all. And, as Fiddes is quick to point out, an appreciation of relationships within God as Trinity would also lead to more emphasis on mutuality. A new emphasis on mutual relationships, inspired by Fiddes' understanding of God as Trinity, has the potential to address the asymmetric relationships that have become normal between disabled and non-disabled people, and the promise of new creative relationships could open up.

Fiddes explores two dimensions of God's intentions for covenant relationships, the 'vertical' and the 'horizontal.' In some accounts, this has almost sounded like two distinct covenants.[180] Such a

---

[178] Peter Oakes suggests that in Galatians 3:26-29 Paul is arguing for unity within diversity, see his commentary *Galatians* (Grand Rapids, MI: Baker, 2015), 127-32.

[179] John Swinton, (ed.) *Critical Reflections on Stanley Hauerwas' Theology of Disability: Disabling Society, Enabling Theology* (New York, Oxford: Routledge, 2004), 7 quoting Frances M. Young, *Face to Face: A Narrative Essay in the Theology of Suffering* (Edinburgh: T & T Clark, 1990), 192, paraphrasing Gal 3:28 and Col 3:11.

[180] For example, Leon McBeth, 'Baptist Church Covenants', *Baptist*

separation would wrongly suggest a divide between God's covenant initiative with all creation and our covenant relationships with each other. This could lead to all kinds of unhelpful scenarios and seriously limit the way in which we understand God's desire to be in covenant with all people. If, for example, the reality on the ground is that disabled people are denied full covenant relationships with others in a church community, it is hard to separate this from the implication that God has different desires for relationships with disabled and non-disabled people.

An understanding of covenant relationships that sees them as manifestations of God's covenant relationship with the world has the potential to foster inclusion and participation well beyond the local church congregation. If congregations understand themselves to be in strong covenant relationships with other churches, the local Association, and the wider Union of churches, then good practice concerning inclusion is more likely to be shared, and individuals are more likely to be encouraged to participate in wider church life. That was certainly my own experience during the process of testing a call to ministry. The church in which I was a member at the time had good relationships with other Baptist churches and the local Association. This

---

History and Heritage 27.1 (1992) suggests, falsely, that confessional documents are about the vertical, while covenant documents are about the horizontal, contra the fact that in the seventeenth century they were often in one document. Although Hayden suggests that the two aspects were considered to be very different relationships, Roger Hayden, 'The Particular Baptist Confession 1689 and Baptists Today', *Baptist Quarterly* 32.8 (1988): 413.

assisted in the provision of opportunities for me to preach and lead services beyond the local congregation and facilitated my involvement in the local Association. Although the language of covenant was not widely used at the time, there is little doubt that my experience was a practical outworking of an open understanding of covenant relationships beyond the local congregation.

Friendship and Baptist Covenant Communities

In this final section, I want to suggest that friendship, understood in terms of being intentional, mutual and particular, has the potential to foster participatory inclusion of disabled people. Within Baptist church communities, these friendships can be understood in terms of our covenant relationship with God, one another, and the world.[181]

Friendships exist within a continuum of relationships, ranging from the most intimate to the most hostile. Sally McFague refers to this as the 'sliding definition of a friend.'[182] Hostile relationships, for example, between opposing members of street

---

[181] Toth, 'From the Love of Friends', 74 argues for the importance of friendship with church communities, despite the ambivalence of some theologians.

[182] Stephen Summers, *Friendship: Exploring Its Implications for the Church in Postmodernity* (London: T & T Clark, 2009), 72; Werner G. Jeanrond, *A Theology of Love* (London: T & T Clark, 2010), 205; Sallie McFague, *Metaphorical Theology: Models of God in Religious Language* (London: SCM, 1983), 157.

gangs, show no signs of friendship whatsoever. These would be examples of highly distorted relationships that restrict the possibilities of personhood for the individuals involved.[183] Relationships that range from the intimacy of a long-term marriage to the more distant, casual and transitory provide different levels of intensity and inclusion between individuals and groups, which can be understood in terms of friendships.[184] These are relationships that undistort the personhood of those involved.[185] For some time now, virtual friendships through social media have become commonplace and now need to be included within the continuum, although they stretch beyond the scope of this chapter.[186]

There are three basic themes that have emerged in the long history of writing about the nature of friendship.[187] There is general

---

[183] A. I. McFadyen, *The Call to Personhood: A Christian Theory of the Individual in Social Relationships* (Cambridge: Cambridge University Press, 1990), 42.

[184] Liz Spencer and R. E. Pahl, *Rethinking Friendship: Hidden Solidarities Today* (Princeton, NJ: Princeton University Press, 2006) discussed by Summers, *Friendship*, 72.

[185] McFadyen, *The Call to Personhood*, 45.

[186] Barbro Fröding and Martin Peterson, 'Why Virtual Friendship Is No Genuine Friendship', *Ethics and Information Technology* 14.3 (2012); Karen Stendal, 'How Do People with Disability Use and Experience Virtual Worlds and ICT: A Literature Review', *Journal for Virtual Worlds Research* 5.1 (2012) discuss the impact of virtual relationships for disabled people. Summers, *Friendship*, 31-5 comments on the range of relationships which include virtual ones.

[187] Paul J. Wadell, *Becoming Friends: Worship, Justice, and the Practice*

agreement that friendships are good and beneficial for those involved, often by placing the good of the other before self. It has been recognised as important, however, that friendships should be reciprocal and mutual, with both self and other contributing to and receiving from the friendship. There has been discussion about the relative merits of friendships between just two people and friendships that are more inclusive. Although friendships have often been thought of as being essentially private, they are able to be effective in the public realm. Friendships may differ if they are based on intrinsic or extrinsic factors. Friendships based on intrinsic factors, such as mutual attraction or liking, tend to require a level of similarity. Friendships grounded extrinsically in the acknowledgement of God's universal love, however, have the potential to enable relationships to form between people who have significant differences.

Friendship, recognised as an expression of God's universal love, is the best way to nurture relationships between disabled and non-disabled people in the context of Baptist communities. My hope would be that Baptist communities can play a part in helping people move from highly distorted asymmetric relationships to less distorted mutual relationships. This should, in turn, enable people to move away from impersonal, so-called 'I-It' relationships towards more inclusive 'I-Thou' relationships.

---

of Christian Friendship (Grand Rapids, MI: Brazos, 2002), 39-66; Friendship and the Moral Life (Notre Dame: University of Notre Dame Press, 1989), 97-104; Guido de Graaff, Politics in Friendship: A Theological Account (London: Bloomsbury, 2014), 11-16.

There are parallels between the shift from an Individual/Medical Model of Disability to Social Models of Disability and the discovery of friendship. When people form friendships with others, the focus of attention moves from the self, often in isolation, to the other and the importance of the relationship. This resonates with a more general shift from 'centred-self', a concept that has held considerable influence throughout the period we think of as modernity, towards the concept of a 'de-centred self', which has become more prevalent in late-modernity.[188] A core feature of the de-centred self is a radical openness to the other, welcoming meaningful relationships that embrace difference rather than homogeneity.[189] There are, however, risks in de-centring, the most significant of which is extreme individualism of the kind that denies interrelatedness. These can be mitigated within a Christian context if it is also understood that the shift away from self-centredness can simultaneously be a shift towards a Christ-centred self.[190] This is a very different form of 'connected-self', in which the self is understood in terms of being profoundly related and in real dialogue with another. As Summers says, 'relationship with the other is an integral part of who the self is.'[191]

---

[188] Summers, *Friendship*, 112-16.

[189] Summers, *Friendship*, 116-17.

[190] Bill Gaventa, 'From Strangers to Friends: A New Testament Call to Community', *Journal of Religion, Disability & Health* 16.2 (2012) connects the New Testament understanding of the significance of friendship with the inclusion of disabled people.

[191] Summers, *Friendship*, 113-14.

The specific characteristics of friendship have been much debated, but for the purpose of fostering the inclusion of disabled people in Baptist church communities, I want to focus on three aspects mentioned earlier. Firstly, such friendships need to be intentional, in formation and in purpose. Friendships between disabled and non-disabled people need to be intentionally formed to overcome the perceived differences between people that tend to inhibit the formation of friendships. They also need to have the explicit purpose of including one another. This intentionality addresses the exclusion from relationships and participation that disabled people have historically experienced. I noted earlier that intentionality was also a feature of covenant-making within and between Baptist congregations.

Secondly, these friendships need to explicitly emphasise mutuality between disabled and non-disabled participants. This emphasis is important to challenge the experience of asymmetric relationships that assume carer/cared for roles for non-disabled and disabled people, respectively. There is a long history of disabled peoples' lives being controlled by those in the medical and related caring professions. As noted earlier, there is evidence that this approach has led to an impoverished pastoral care approach being taken towards disabled people within church communities. By emphasising the mutuality of friendships, the contribution of each person, disabled or non-disabled, is valued as much as the benefit gained from receiving from the relationship. The focus on mutuality was identified above as a characteristic of Baptist understandings of covenant relationships.

Thirdly, these friendships are particular. This does not mean that they are exclusive friendships between particular people but that they are friendships that take into account the particularity of the participants and their contexts. While the Individual/Medical Model of Disability overemphasised the individual, the Social Model of Disability overcompensated by focusing on the general relationships and actions of society towards 'the disabled'. The nature of disability is complex, and the experiences of disabled people are significantly influenced by many factors, as indicated at the beginning of this chapter. Friendships have the potential to take these multiple factors into account. This enables disabled and non-disabled people to seek participatory inclusion in their specific contexts in ways that may be very different for other contexts and other people. This is a reflection of the emphasis among Baptists on the particular significance of a local congregation and its context.

Conclusion

One of the most significant reasons that disabled people have historically been excluded from society and from church communities has been the dominance of the Individual/Medical Model of Disability. This located the 'problem of disability' with individuals and required them to change or be cured/healed in order to participate in society. If this was not possible, then they were institutionalised or viewed as passive recipients of pastoral care, leading to isolation and loneliness. The change in understanding of disability brought about by the development of the Social Models of Disability in the late twentieth century located the 'problem of disability' with societal attitudes and actions towards disabled people. This change facilitated greater inclusion in society but largely ignored the importance of inter-personal relationships. By focussing on relationships with the Trinity and our participatory covenantal relationship with God and other believers, the nature of relationships between disabled and non-disabled people comes to the fore. If these are understood in terms of friendships which are intentional, mutual and particular, then there is the potential to foster greater participatory inclusion within Baptist church communities locally, within association life and that of Baptists Together. Such friendships also have the potential to make a difference beyond Baptist and other church communities, challenging a pastoral mode of disability which assumes disabled people are passive. Meaningful friendships between disabled and non-disabled people can help address the isolation and loneliness that is the experience of many disabled people. Such a change would be a sign of the Kingdom of God being made a reality in our local congregations and communities.

5   Can we Talk? A Reflection on Baptists Together and Equal Marriage

Pam Davies

In 2022, two different letters, signed by Baptist Ministers and members, were submitted to the Baptist Council, one of which advocated for the adoption of equal marriage for Baptist Ministers as church practice and one which did not. The traction these two documents have gained has led to one of the most damaging misconceptions in Baptist circles today, that the issue of equal marriage is polarised. There are two initial problems with this statement. Firstly, healthy conversations are not facilitated in an environment within which entire people groups are considered a problem. Those within Baptist communities cannot and should not describe people, their relationships, and their identities as an 'issue.' People are not an issue or a problem to be solved; they are a gift. The recognition of the inherent value of the individual is our starting point.

Secondly, the concept of polarisation introduces an 'us and them' mentality. This chapter does not seek to explore how Baptists might engage with LGBTQ+ communities because numerous Baptist expressions of faith already include and affirm LGBTQ+ members, many of whom have expressed commitment to their partner through equal marriage. This means that ours is not a conversation within which the heterosexual Christian seeks to

111

engage with the LGBTQ+ nonbeliever. A question that much better encapsulates the current context in which we all seek to serve God is this: can we, as a collection of thousands of different expressions of faith, end the silence at congregational level to meaningfully explore whether we can hold together the multitude of understandings of marriage across Baptists Together in a way that is healthy, covenantal, and gracious? Beyond this, can we do so in a manner that sets our benchmark as not merely the absence of harm but the cultivation of an environment where all can thrive?

Where to Start?

In 2019/20, I undertook a small study facilitating conversations between affirming and non-affirming[192] Christians while separately surveying the views of Baptist Ministers across one Association. The purpose of this interaction was not to bring readers or participants to an amalgamated viewpoint but to consider how LGBTQ+ voices might be introduced to a conversation that has historically excluded them.

The findings from the focus groups and surveys shared in this chapter seek to offer a described reality of the current climate within Baptists Together, which might not only offer a context for theological reflection but one within which the practices are recognised as 'embodiments of faith seeking understanding: they

---

[192] Specifically, those who celebrated equal marriage and those who did not.

form a theological voice [among others], or authority, which needs to be listened to as such.'[193] Recognising that there are varied contributors to this conversation enables the church to engage as one conversation partner among many, through the commonality of particularity. This is a necessity when exploring a subject shaped not only by scripture, theology, and ecclesiology but by a number of additional partners, including culture, lived experience and government legislation, to name only a few.

While initially helpful, the aim of producing a 'described reality' also creates several issues. Claire Watkins warns that new ecclesiology is at risk of producing 'descriptions of the living church,'[194] while remaining 'at a loss as to what to make of the described realities theologically.'[195] Description alone is insufficient, therefore, we will move beyond this, once we have identified the tensions that exist between affirming and non-affirming Baptists, to consider whether there might be grounds for reconciling them.

A further challenge is highlighted by Boeve, who cautions that 'a theological investigation raising theological questions from the very start... interrupts a straightforward appeal to continuity or

---

[193] Claire Watkins, 'Practising Ecclesiology: From Product to Process: Developing Ecclesiology as a Non-Correlative Process and Practice through the Theological Action Research Framework of Theology in Four Voices', *Ecclesial Practices* 2.1 (2015), 35.

[194] Watkins, 'Practising Ecclesiology', 24.

[195] Watkins, 'Practising Ecclesiology', 24.

discontinuity.'[196] This is a helpful reflection for any conversation that takes place within the non-hierarchical structures of Baptists Together and requires an openness to engaging with views and experiences outside of our own. This means that the nuanced nature of theological discussion must be protected, with its variety of contributors and influences. Helpfully, Cameron and Duce explain that, 'the goal... is not to reach a consensus.'[197] Our purpose is not to impose a centralised perspective on the entirety of Baptists Together (an impossibility in itself) but to create opportunities for us to listen well, acknowledge interpretations of scripture and lived experiences that differ from our own and to care wholeheartedly for those God has called and entrusted to us.

What do Baptists Believe?

Following Baptist Assembly in 2013, three majority views on equal marriage were identified. These views were recorded as 'those who hold to a traditional line, those who want to hold to a traditional line but are struggling for words to be true to their pastoral concerns; and those who are prepared to accept.'[198] These clear, seemingly opposing views are considered here as 'inherited, pastoral and affirming.' These headings are adopted in

---

[196] Lieven Boeve, 'Mutual Interruption Toward a Positive Tension between Theology and Religious Studies', *Louvain Studies* 34 (2010), 14.

[197] Helen Cameron, and Catherine Duce *Ministry and Mission: A Companion* (SCM Press: London, 2013), 109.

[198] https://www.baptist.org.uk/Articles/525805/Talking_Together_discussion .aspx

recognition of the limitations of language and seek only to convey a distinctive feature of each view for the purposes of identifying differing perspectives. It should be acknowledged that holders of both inherited and affirming views do so while maintaining a desire to be pastoral, that the term inherited intends to convey a sense of historical Baptist understandings of LQBTQ+ relationships and does not attempt to suggest that those who hold such a view have not considered it for themselves while affirming specifically refers to the practice of equal marriage in this context. Since each position can be justified in scripture, the term 'biblical' has been intentionally avoided, and 'traditional' has been amended to 'inherited' since Anderson argues that 'a conservative guess is that 98% of our behaviour is rooted in one tradition or another.'[199] These three headings are well-matched with three of Elmes' five Christian views on LGBTQ+ relationships, the relevant parts of which are quoted below.[200] While these were the most widely held views of those who participated in the research, it is noteworthy that they are included as an indicator of the present landscape and do not encourage a democratic approach to inclusion, which would be inconsistent with Baptist ecclesiology since discernment requires greater engagement than simply the adoption of the existing majority view.

---

[199] Leith Anderson, *Church for the 21st Century* (Grand Rapids, MI: Bethany House, 1992), 146.

[200] Steve Elmes, *Sexuality, Faith and the Art of Conversation: Part One* (Surrey: Creative Tension Publications, 2017), 21.

On discernment in a broader sense, Andy Goodliff describes a way forward when the local church is unable to communicate being 'of one mind' on a particular conversation, explaining the possibility of finding 'a way of living with that tension and those differences and that difficulty because our way of understanding baptism and the church meeting allows us to do that. But we're always seeking it, we're always asking the question, "what is Christ saying?".'

The Inherited View

'Scripture condemns homosexual practice and the church should always regard it as sinful. Furthermore, sexual attraction to someone of the same sex should be repented of and healing sought from such desires.'[201] People who maintain this view 'conserve and live by their understanding of transcendent truth.'[202] Because these values are 'culturally transcendent' and founded in scripture, there is no process by which individual believers adopt their own, rather the expectation is that believers who hold the inherited view will assume a pre-existing moral structure. This position generally advocates a literal interpretation of scripture, with references to texts such as 'man shall not lie with man' (Lev

---

[201] Elmes, *Sexuality, Faith and the Art of Conversation*, 21.

[202] David R. Hodge, 'Epistemological Frameworks, Homosexuality and Religion: How People of Faith Understand the Intersection Between Homosexuality and Religion,' *Social Work* 50.3 (2005): 207.

18.22) and 'men committed shameful acts with other men, and received in themselves the due penalty for their error' (Rom 1.27), providing a biblical foundation for the rejection of equal marriage as church practice.

This position, like the two that follow it, is contested. Melendez and LaSala write, 'there are numerous historical examples that absolute transcendent truths and values have varied by time period and cultural context.'[203] Examples of the Baptist response to historic issues of justice, such as slavery and the ordination of women, both demonstrate occasions on which the transcendent value has been shaped by lived experience. While the subjects of complementarianism and egalitarianism continue to prompt conversation among some Baptist churches in the twenty-first century, the structures within the movement celebrate the ordination of women and the abolishment of slavery. In addition to this, the inherited position presents issues when different faith communities hold differing values; namely that if absolute, transcendent truth is sought, then which has discerned the mind of Christ accurately?

The Pastoral View

The biblical norm from Creation onwards is marriage between a man and a woman, and no alternative is envisaged apart from

---

[203] Michael P. Melendez and Michael C. LaSala, 'Who's Oppressing Whom? Homosexuality, Christianity, and Social Work,' *Social Work* 51.4 (2006): 373.

celibacy. . . . At the same time, great care should be taken to avoid putting pressure on those who are homosexual to seek and experience change in their sexual orientation, as this typically brings more feelings of guilt than healing.[204]

This view neither accepts nor affirms LGBTQ+ relationships but does articulate that every individual is deserving of appropriate pastoral care and that such care should not take the form of conversion therapy (which organisations such as Stonewall and One Body One Faith, among others, are calling for the British government to ban as a result of the harm it is demonstrated to have caused and continues to cause).[205]

According to this viewpoint, the importance of effective pastoral care cannot be underestimated, with Griffin writing that those who experience it can move from 'the feelings of shame and guilt and low self-esteem to a state of peace.'[206] However, this approach does raise the question as to how effective pastoral care can be when the body providing it does not offer full acceptance to the recipient.

---

[204] Elmes, *Sexuality, Faith and the Art of Conversation*, 22.

[205] https://www.stonewall.org.uk/about-us/news/ban-conversion-therapy-why-we-need-ban-no-exemptions-and-no-excuses

[206] Horace L. Griffin, 'Revisioning Christian Ethical Discourse on Homosexuality: A Challenge for Pastoral Care in the 21st Century', *Journal of Pastoral Care* 53.2 (1999): 216.

The Affirming View

'What scripture affirms everywhere is covenant loyalty, and this is given its clearest affirmation in marriage (between a man and a woman). However, it can also be expressed in faithful, loving and monogamous homosexual partnerships.'[207]

One of the scriptural justifications for affirming theology is partly based on the, perhaps indecipherable, New Testament term *arsenokoites*, which references abusive imbalances of sexual power. The word, 'hadn't occurred in any previous documents,' and was perhaps 'coined' by Paul.[208] Since *arsenokoites* cannot be accurately translated there was potential for Vicky Beeching (among others), who documents a personal change in understanding of scripture, that the meaning of Paul's writings on homosexuality (1 Cor 6:9-10 and 1 Tim 1:8-11) may have been mistranslated.[209] This approach deals with challenging Old Testament texts by examining the historical contexts of the writings and would state, for example, that the account of Sodom and Gomorrah was an issue of hospitality rather than sexuality and that New Testament writings reference pederasty rather than consensual, loving, same-sex relationships.[210]

---

[207] Elmes, *Sexuality, Faith and the Art of Conversation*, 22.

[208] Vicky Beeching, *Undivided: Coming Out, Becoming Whole and Living Free from Shame* (London: Harper Collins, 2018), 85.

[209] As in 1 Corinthians 6:9-10 and 1 Timothy 1:8-11.

[210] Robert K. Gnuse, 'Seven Gay Texts: Biblical Passages Used to Condemn Homosexuality,' *Biblical Theology Bulletin* 45.2 (2015): 75.

This position is challenged by a more literalist view, which would argue that scripture is clear on the subject of equal marriage, quoting verses such a Leviticus 18:22, which Sphero responds to by asserting that the Holiness code no longer applies.[211] Each position is in agreement over the wording of scripture; what is challenged or explored across these varied understandings is the broader context and intended meaning behind each text.

Reflections

The self-selecting group of Ministers who participated in the survey could all identify their theological view within this range. 48% held a pastoral view of equal marriage, 41% held an affirming view of equal marriage, and 9% held an inherited view of equal marriage. Non-affirming members who contributed to the focus group sessions were also able to identify their theological view within this range as being inherited, pastoral or a blend of both. LGBTQ+ contributors, however, were unable to find their theology reflected in these interpretations of equal marriage, stating that the affirming view 'still seems a bit reserved, a bit binary, it doesn't go quite as far as I'd like it to go.'[212] Another participant observed that the definition suggested 'hetero-superiority' and offered a 'rigid point of view,' with

---

[211] M. W. Sphero, *The Gay Faith: Christ, Scripture and Sexuality* (New Orleans: Hermes, 2011), 42.

[212] Focus Group Transcript.

'negative connotations for same-sex married couples.'[213] A further participant reflected, 'if you see the three categories as a scale then my own personal opinion would be further along the scale than that one.'[214]

The absence of marginalised voices in conversation thus far means that an unequal platform has been created for LGBTQ+ Christians who might otherwise be prepared to contribute to theological reflection on this subject. Group reflection demonstrates that LGBTQ+ participants do not enter into conversations about marriage on equal footing with their heterosexual peers. While this was anticipated in terms of additional requirements around pastoral care, the findings that entire theologies are absent and unsuitable language has become normalised[215] further demonstrate that consequences of the inherited / pastoral theologies are far-reaching, beyond the question of whether or not equal marriage might be permitted or encouraged in local church contexts. There appears to be no documented awareness of what LGBTQ+ people believe about sexuality or what appropriate language might be.

---

[213] Focus Group Transcript.

[214] Focus Group Transcript.

[215] Specifically, the reference to 'homosexual genital practice' in the Baptist Union's Ministerial Recognition Rules.

What Shapes a View?

Now we have established that there is an extensive range of views held across the breadth of Baptists Together, demonstrated through reflections from Ministers and members, we can move on to consider some of the factors that have shaped these positions. We continue with the understanding that capturing every unique theology within the constraints of this chapter is an impossibility and that there are a considerable number of views that cannot be captured in a study of this size.

As Christians, scripture seems a sensible starting point. This was reported by participants as having varied influences on their theological stance. The repetitive term in each statement from LGBTQ+ contributors was guidance, with scripture being described as a set of transferable principles, whereas non-affirming, heterosexual group members adopted a more literal approach. All group members were able to recognise that their hermeneutics influenced their understanding of marriage to varying extents. For example, one person who affirmed equal marriage explained, 'scripture hasn't influenced my view on same sex marriage, apart from God being all loving,'[216] while another LGBTQ+ participant approached things slightly differently by using Jesus as a reference point. 'I would want to see how Jesus was, and I would want to be Jesus-like, as opposed to looking at a specific quote and living by it.'[217] Another suggested, 'it's more

---

[216] Focus Group Transcript.
[217] Focus Group Transcript.

about what I learnt from the bible about who God is and what I learnt from the bible about what love is that helped me to come to this position of being affirming and believing that all people should be able to get married.'[218] Each of these approaches is more reliant on the overarching characteristics of God rather than those expressed through a specific text. While this approach might not adopt the predominant approach to hermeneutics, it is noteworthy that this lens of God's character (expressed, in part, through the metanarrative of scripture) is no less theological than the tools adopted by those who maintain an inherited view. A hierarchy of hermeneutics, which prioritises one method of interpretation over others, is unable to fully account for the many ways that God chooses to relate to God's people.

The non-affirming view held by others in the group was based on the 'principle of first occurrence.'[219] According to this view, 'both male and female, in a complementary way, give children, and therefore the whole of society, the clearest picture of the character of God. So that's the basis of whichever he's built.'[220] This was reflected in another view, shaped by Genesis 2:24, 'God's design was for marriage, and he didn't leave room for same sex marriage and that still would be my position.'[221]

---

[218] Focus Group Transcript.

[219] Focus Group Transcript.

[220] Focus Group Transcript.

[221] Focus Group Transcript.

The parallels thus far are interesting, each LGBTQ+ participant held a 'beyond affirming' view of sexuality[222], a hermeneutic of 'original meaning,'[223] and a willingness to adopt equal marriage as church practice. One member observed,

> Time and time again it seems to suggest the relationships that they were referring to [in scripture] were not loving, committed, romantic and selfless relationships, like a couple. They seem to be referring to lustful and often abusive, non-consensual, or where there's a massive age difference or a power thing, it's disgraceful for a man to have sex with someone of a lower status unless they're the active part in that.

In contrast, non-affirming, heterosexual participants maintained a combination of inherited and pastoral views of sexuality, a literal hermeneutic, an unwillingness to adopt equal marriage as church practice and an understanding of marriage shaped by commitment and covenant. One participant suggested, 'the basis of marriage is not love, the basis of marriage is commitment, really.'[224]

The movement from one of these viewpoints to another is significant because it is not solely a question of affirming equal marriage as an isolated practice. Thompson depicts nine different

---

[222] Stating that the affirming view was unable to capture their theology.

[223] Judith Thompson, *Theological Reflection* (SCM Press: London, 2016), 76.

[224] Focus Group Transcript.

methods of interpretation of scripture in the Judeo-Christian tradition and each of these shapes how one might respond to the gift of marriage.[225] Additionally, Hunter describes two predominant worldviews which also influence the position a person might hold. These views, 'orthodox,' and 'progressive'[226] are not formed in the context of religious belief but as a 'formal [property] of a belief system or worldview.'[227] He continues that within cultural progressivism, 'moral authority tends to be defined by the spirit of the modern age, a spirit of rationalism and subjectivism.'[228] This allows moral authority to be shaped by lived experience and renders truth 'a reality that is ever unfolding.'[229] In contrast, the orthodox view emphasises 'a commitment on the part of adherents to an external, definable and transcendent authority.'[230] This brings a broader awareness of the conversations around equal marriage. While clearly shaped by Baptist ecclesiology, which is informed by scripture, Hunter warns against viewing the culture wars as 'merely the accumulation of social issues debated today.'[231] This demonstrates that worldview and hermeneutics both play a significant role in the formation of an individuals' affirmation or

---

[225] Thompson, *Theological Reflection*, 76.

[226] James Davison Hunter, *Culture Wars: The Struggle to Define America* (New York: HarperCollins, 1991), 43.

[227] Hunter, *Culture Wars*, 44.

[228] Focus Group Transcript.

[229] Focus Group Transcript.

[230] Focus Group Transcript.

[231] Hunter, *Culture Wars*, 48.

rejection of equal marriage, in addition to their understanding of the boundaries of ecclesiology. Sustaining awareness of these differing worldviews and hermeneutical approaches and attempting to capture them has assisted with this research by helping participants understand why they might hold a particular view.

The primary concern raised by most respondents who espoused a non-affirming view of equal marriage in both the focus groups and survey responses was the tension between contemporary practice and scripture. It is helpful to recognise that those who held a non-affirming position expressed a sincere attempt to adhere to a particular understanding of marriage; how this position might be held in a way that does not unintentionally cause pain is something that is considered further on.

It is also noteworthy that not every member of the LGBTQ+ community is supportive of equal marriage. Ettelbrick writes emotively on the potentially negative consequences of its introduction, 'ironically, gay marriage, instead of liberating gay sex and sexuality, would further outlaw all gay and lesbian sex which is not performed in a marital context.'[232] This highlights that any suggestion that the present disagreement is between LGBTQ+ and heterosexual Christians is reductionist and inaccurate. While these categorisations attempt to capture the three majority views identified in previous research carried out by

---

[232] Paula Ettelbrick, *Since When is Marriage a Path to Liberation?* (Outlook: National Gay and Lesbian Quarterly, 1993), 403.

Baptists Together, as well as those held by LGBTQ+ contributors who could not find their theologies recorded, there are a limitless number of views maintained on an individual level by people of all sexualities and identities.

The Role of the Local Church

Churches have responded to this extensive range of views in different ways. 80% of the Ministers surveyed recorded that they had engaged in conversations with their leadership teams about equal marriage, whereas only 45% of Ministers had initiated conversations with the wider church. It may be the case that the perception of this as a polarising conversation has discouraged churches from engaging in discussion about equal marriage on a wider level, and the desire to prevent a local church split would explain the significant difference in engagement at leadership and congregational levels. Despite this, the responses present a challenge to us: how many churches hold a developed, considered theology that has been discerned by the membership in contrast with those who have simply adopted the theology of their Minister or leadership team? The latter would not appear to be compatible with the 'liberty to discern' outlined in the Baptist Union's Declaration of Principle, which is extended to the body of the church rather than a privileged few, regardless of how well-intentioned the motives of the church leadership team may be. Of the churches that did engage in theological reflection about equal marriage, less than 10% actively invited LGBTQ+ individuals to contribute to their discussions. There appears to be a constriction within Baptist churches whereby Ministers form their theology, and church leadership teams are often, but not always, invited to reflect on this view. Commonly, the wider membership is not invited to this conversation, which largely does not involve representation from the marginalised communities whom the conversation most affects. 80% of Ministers felt that the church they serve had the liberty to discern for themselves whether they should introduce equal marriage, which is significant in light of the number of churches that did not make a decision by way of the church meeting, with those who felt they did not have liberty appealing to scripture for the justification of a non-affirming view.

This silence at a congregational level has had a significant impact on LGBTQ+ contributors to this research, who described the accompanying fear they experienced within their respective local church settings. One participant shared the uncertainty they experienced being in an environment where equal marriage had never been discussed, despite several requests having been made by LGBTQ+ members. 'It is that silence from some that, there was a person who was like, "I thought we were inclusive," and actually, no-one's ever spoken about it, so no-one knows. It's that silence where LGBT young people, and people anywhere just go, "what if they hate me?"'[233]

Another highlighted the contrast between how Christians and non-Christians responded,

---

[233] Focus Group Transcript.

I found a divide between Christian friends and family and non-Christian friends and family. All my Christian friends and families' responses were negative and all my non-Christian friends and families' responses were positive. It made me feel angry at Christians. I am a Christian too, it made me feel annoyed that the group I was part of was the scariest group to tell.[234]

Only one person shared a positive experience from their local (affirming) church, explaining, 'it was my Christian friends and a Christian community and church that actually helped me through that process of starting to be open. Now that's where I feel safest to be myself, and it's a Christian community.'[235]

Interestingly, one contributor who maintained a non-affirming view offered their own experience of isolation within their respective setting, stating 'most churches, if they disagree with something, they don't argue they just ostracise you... you can get pushed out of a church.'[236] This highlighted a lived experience of one member attempting to hold the tension between their inherited viewpoint and the more affirming theology adopted by the local church they were a part of.

Regardless of theological position, the group unanimously expressed the importance of effective pastoral care, which offers

---

[234] Focus Group Transcript.

[235] Focus Group Transcript.

[236] Focus Group Transcript.

a helpful starting point for future conversations. Reflection on the Ozanne Foundation's research into mental health among LGBTQ+ Christians prompted a shared understanding that the church, no matter its theology, maintains a responsibility to the LGBTQ+ community in regard to pastoral care.[237]

> I feel like, no matter where you stand, we all have to do something to stop people like committing suicide or starving themselves or having these awful mental health conditions as a result of their treatment by the church. You don't have to be affirming to agree with that, that people deserve to not be driven to desperate measures.[238]

Those who held a non-affirming view agreed with this sentiment while maintaining a non-affirming view,

> I certainly feel much more could and should be done. I also would say, and I would say respectfully, you don't do that by changing your beliefs because truth is truth and you can't just dilute it because it's convenient to do that, which is what I think modern culture is trying to do.[239]

The group reflected that pastoral care did not have to be dependent on uniformity of view but that the need to care for LGBTQ+

---

[237] The Ozanne Foundation, *Executive Summary: Faith and Sexuality Survey 2018.*

[238] Focus Group Transcript.

[239] Focus Group Transcript.

members existed regardless of the varying theologies that were present. 'I think the issue is not entirely that we should just have like a homogenous view, it's that whatever our views, our pastoral care needs to be better.'[240]

Membership

While we have identified so far that the church can, and should, facilitate healthy, whole-church conversations and provide suitable pastoral care to LGBTQ+ members, focus group sessions also highlighted that the feared 'split' that might be prompted by conversations about equal marriage has, arguably, already taken place.

LGBTQ+ participants had all either joined or moved to faith communities which practice equal marriage. Equally, those who held the inherited or pastoral positions had either joined or moved to faith communities which do not practice equal marriage, with one contributor having made the decision to move to a different faith community as a direct result of their church adopting a more affirming understanding of marriage. When asked whether group members might consider it feasible to join a church where the practice was in conflict with their own views, all but one of the respondents answered 'no. 'LGBTQ+ members raised concerns about identity, acceptance, and membership, stating,

---

[240] Focus Group Transcript.

Being a queer person in my church, if that was an inherited model of church and they didn't believe that I should marry, I couldn't exist there fully content and fully peaceful because I would always feel that my membership was half of what everyone else's was.[241]

Another reflected, 'maybe I would feel different in a church that had said that "we've discussed it and we know it's important but it's not something we agree with," but I can't say that I personally would feel comfortable in that church.'[242] The final respondent offered a slightly different view, but expressed significant reservations, 'I think as long as I wasn't having someone to shout "repent", at me, I think if it wasn't made such a massive thing, then *maybe*.'[243]

Perhaps one of the reasons that Ministers have not, thus far, initiated whole-church conversations about equal marriage is due to fear of division. While well-intentioned, the focus group has highlighted the painful consequences of silence alongside the exclusion that is experienced when churches refuse to outline their position, despite the fact that conversation actively encouraged healthy relationships rather than causing further damage. In fact, while this approach identified areas of deep disagreement, it also highlighted areas of consensus. Equal marriage as church practice is disputed, and interpretations of scripture are broad; however,

---

[241] Focus Group Transcript.
[242] Focus Group Transcript.
[243] Focus Group Transcript.

the autonomy of the local church and the requirement for comprehensive pastoral care for LGBTQ+ believers generated consensus in both the focus group sessions and the wider survey of Ministers. Perhaps future conversation might develop by drawing on these areas of shared understanding rather than considering areas of division as a starting point.

Those who maintained the inherited / pastoral viewpoints appreciated the vulnerability of LGBTQ+ contributors. Despite maintaining a non-affirming theology of equal marriage, they fed back that, 'I've been really quite shocked by some things that [have been] said about the vulnerability of your community. How vilified and hated they've been, I've really been quite shocked by that and very, very sad.'[244] A second appreciated the insight of those who experience church differently,

> At least we can hear what the other person says which I think has been a good thing. The mental health thing, which I've always been aware of, but you've reminded me, of the stigma and the rejection and so forth are far bigger issues than then those of us who are heterosexual, middle class or the rest of it, wouldn't normally get.[245]

LGBTQ+ contributors offered similar insights in terms of hearing an alternate perspective. One stated, 'it has really surprised me as well how many different ways there are to think differently about

---

[244] Focus Group Transcript.
[245] Focus Group Transcript.

this.'[246] Another felt, 'you often only hear people are on the same side as you. I don't want to call it 'sides' because that's very divisive... I'm interested to hear that side of the story.'[247] The final participant found group interaction helpful, particularly having discussed in former sessions numerous failed attempts to encourage their local church to initiate conversations about sexuality, 'I think it's been good to have an open conversation about it all, because people don't. In that way it's been interesting, how we can talk about it, it's a new experience isn't it really?'[248]

Introducing previously neglected voices to conversations about equal marriage, contrary to causing further division, created a new appreciation for differing perspectives. While nobody changed their theology of marriage, the group was united in the benefits of conversation as well as the need for suitable pastoral care for LGBTQ+ Christians. One group member summarised the usefulness of conversation as follows, 'when you sit down and talk to people on a one to one or small group like we are, you get a much more human face than the, as I said before, across the battle lines in a church meeting, that sort of thing. And I think maybe there's a way forward there.'[249]

---

[246] Focus Group Transcript.

[247] Focus Group Transcript.

[248] Focus Group Transcript.

[249] Focus Group Transcript.

To avoid the earlier trap outlined by Watkins, we must move beyond the description of the present landscape and theologically reflect on what this means for the Baptist movement. As a collection of differing bodies, not limited to local churches, colleges, and associations, we can turn to Paul Fiddes' reflections on covenant theology, which offer us a helpful way forward. Covenant in a Baptist context is unique and highlights the intersection between horizontal and vertical theologies. For example, 'it is only those who are horizontally covenanted to each other, even if only two or three in number, who embody and make actual the authority of Christ, with whom each is individually covenanted in the (vertical) grace of redemption.'[250] The vertical covenant is initiated by God, and through it, humanity participates 'not only in God's covenant with us, but in the inner covenant-making in God.'[251] The inner covenant-making is described by Fiddes as 'the agreement undertaken and signed by church members when a particular local church was founded, and subsequently by new members upon their entering it.'[252]

'Interdependence' is encouraged between the various member bodies of the movement so that each part of the wider collective

---

[250] Richard Kidd (ed.), *Something to Declare: A Study of the Declaration of Principle of the Baptist Union of Great Britain* (Oxford: Whitley, 1996), 8.

[251] Paul S. Fiddes, *Tracks and Traces: Baptist Identity in Church and Theology* (Carlisle: Paternoster, 2003), 80.

[252] Fiddes, *Tracks and Traces*, 29.

has the liberty to exercise its own congregational leadership, although this is not in isolation, and the intention, at least, is that local contexts might make use of the spiritual guidance, experiences, or decision-making processes of others as part of the exercise of their liberty. This has been the intention of the Baptist Union's Declaration of Principle for as long as it has been in existence.

For Baptists, the liberty to discern does not translate as the freedom to withdraw into homogenous communities and isolate from those with whom we disagree. Our ecclesiology does not merely grant us permission to disagree well, it actively encourages us with a 'summons to travel beyond them.'[253] Our starting point is listening to the voices that have not yet been heard:

> In finding the mind of Christ we need to listen to the marginalised, the overlooked, with whom he identifies himself. This is what it means to begin with Christ as the 'sole and absolute authority.'[254]

While participants justified their decision to move to affirming or non-affirming churches based on pastoral need and interpretation

---

[253] Beth Allison-Glenny, Andy Goodliff, Ruth Gouldbourne, Steve Holmes, David Kerrigan, Glen Marshall and Simon Woodman, 'The Courage to be Baptist: A Statement on Baptist Ecclesiology and Human Sexuality', *Baptist Quarterly* 48.1 (January 2017), 4.

[254] Kidd (ed.), *Something to Declare,* 35.

of scripture, this movement is suggestive that 'agreeing to disagree,' while an ecclesiological possibility, is practically improbable without significant intervention. While this activity creates communities that share an aligned view of marriage, homogeneity causes tension with the formal theology of Baptist believers. Covenant theology requires relationship, which cannot be sustained if those holding differing viewpoints form exclusive communities. On the subject of covenant, Fiddes' writes, 'intersecting with the 'vertical' dimension of covenant with God in Christ is the 'horizontal dimension' of the members' commitment to each other.'[255] Baptist ecclesiology encapsulates both dimensions, since, 'the freedom of a local church from external ecclesiastical authority is therefore not based in Enlightenment concepts of the freedom of the individual, or in the self-regulation of a voluntary society, but in the lordship of Christ.'[256] While this emphasises the horizontal dimension as members commit to each other in response to God's call, Fiddes' continues, 'there is a universal reality which exists simultaneously with any local manifestation of it [covenant], just as God's eternal covenant with humankind is simultaneous with the local covenant bond.'[257] The assumption that establishing relationships with other members within a specific registered charity is sufficient in the expression of covenant is to overlook the connection between

---

[255] Paul S. Fiddes, 'Baptist Concepts of the Church and their Antecedents' in *The Oxford Handbook to Ecclesiology* edited by Paul Avis (Oxford: Oxford University Press: 2018), 296.

[256] Fiddes, 'Baptist Concepts of the Church', 301.

[257] Fiddes, 'Baptist Concepts of the Church', 297.

the local and eternal dimensions of covenant theology, which are rooted in Baptist history. One focus group member highlighted their concerns in response to a conversation about the transfer of church membership:

> I think very often that's how church turns out, you go to the church where people more or less go along with your view of the world, whether it's a sort of affirming or a type of politics or not. I guess the problem is you're not going [to] find any church that goes along with all the views you agree with. It does strike me that the church it shouldn't really be about that it should be . . . a microcosm of the Universal Church.[258]

Sam Wells helpfully communicates the consequences of this movement towards the formation of like-minded faith communities:

> We could settle for a polite tolerance, all head off into separate congregations with consistent opinions, and never have to meet someone we disagreed with. But we are gathered here this morning, not because we find Christianity helpful or comforting, but because we believe it is *true*. What we have to offer the world is not a book full of answers but a way of continuing a conversation with God and with one another . . . If we can't all stay in

---

[258] Focus Group Transcript.

the room and talk to each other we're telling the world our gospel isn't true.[259]

Covenant theology reminds us that we are invited into relationship with each other and with God. Group contributions demonstrate a personal desire among participants to enact this in their own lives, and Wells identifies that the ways we care for and relate to each other communicate something profound to those outside of our traditions, movements, and faith in a more general sense. While understandings of marriage differ, there is a clear consensus on the importance of conversation and relationship. On this, Goodliff reflects, 'our disagreements almost always take place in public, and so how we handle them is a witness to the truthfulness of the gospel of Jesus Christ.'[260] Theologies of marriage (shaped by all of the influences previously mentioned) determine the likelihood of LGBTQ+ people, including allies, engaging safely with the Baptist movement; theologies of covenant and association that are outworked through genuine depth of relationship during periods of disagreement determine the likelihood of anyone engaging with the Baptist movement. Our Baptist identity, grounded in faith, invites gentle conversation accompanied by the intention of

---

[259] From a sermon by Sam Wells, given in October 2004 to the congregation at St. Mark's, Newnham, Cambridge and subsequently published in Samuel Wells, *Speaking the Truth: Preaching in a Pluralistic Culture* (Nashville: Abingdon, 2008), 196.

[260] Andy Goodliff, 'The Church is Political: Living with our Disagreements', *Baptist Times* April 2022. For a longer version of this article see Andy Goodliff, 'The Politics of Disagreement in the Body of Christ', *Journal of European Baptist Studies* 23.1 (2023): 39-54.

seeking understanding. Whether we are able to learn from, respect and care for each other, particularly during seasons where theological differences have the potential to define us, communicates something clearly to those who do not share our faith. The nature of communication, therefore, plays a role that holds as much importance as its content.

While covenant theology appeals for the dissolution of isolated, homogenous groupings across the Baptist family, which is supported in scripture since texts including Galatians 3:28 and the reading of the New Testament church as undeniably diverse, both emphasise a breadth of variation in church life, in actuality this appears to be a return towards the idealistic, questionably unattainable nature of blueprint theology. How feasible is it for every expression of every Baptist church to be fully diverse in relation to sexuality? A distinctive feature of Paul's writing in Galatians is that while he does not dispute that differences between people continue to exist, what is abolished is the 'evaluative freight carried by these labels, the encoded distinctions of superiority and inferiority.'[261] On this, Stuart offers the following challenge, 'Galatians 3:28 demands that the burden of proof for exclusion from the ecclesial community and its sacraments must always lie with those who would exclude.'[262]. As a minimum, Baptists, particularly those of us in leadership

---

[261] John Barclay, *Paul and the Gift* (Grand Rapids: MI: Eerdmans, 2015), 397.

[262] Elizabeth Stuart, *Gay and Lesbian Theologies: Repetitions with Critical Difference* (New York: Routledge, 2016), 16.

roles or who carry particular authority to make decisions, must continually challenge the divides which threaten sincere attempts to facilitate conversation.

Association

Conversations between affirming and non-affirming Christians within Baptist settings have highlighted the absence of LGBTQ+ contributions in conversations thus far, the reality of a split in a very practical sense across Baptists Together, the shared view that pastoral care is of primary importance, regardless of theological position and a requirement for a depth of relationship in order to adequately live out our covenant theology. What does all of this mean for Baptists moving forward?

The theologies of both affirming and non-affirming contributors have been aligned through their decision to obtain membership in a community which supports their understanding of the gift of marriage. While covenant theology in the Baptist tradition encourages all believers to be in relationship by way of a theology of association, this creates some clear, practical challenges.

In the concrete actuality of contemporary church life, members have felt pressured into making pastorally influenced decisions, with one group member expressing, 'in an ideal world that [unity] would be lovely, we could just have our different views and live with it but people are being hurt,'[263] and another stating, 'the thing

---

[263] Focus Group Transcript.

141

that's frustrating as an LGBT Christian is that we're not talking about it just to talk about being gay. We're talking about it because people are dying.'[264] The decision made by LGBTQ+ members to relocate has come not as a result of intentional theological reflection on covenant as a foundation of formal Baptist theology, but as a mechanism for survival. The treatment of this contribution as a valued theological voice is a necessity in conversation; the relationships required as a holistic expression of covenant become an impossibility when an entire people group are mentally and pastorally unable to endure them.

While there is a clear pastoral need within the current structures of Baptists Together for safe spaces to exist, LGBTQ+ participants identified the danger of their formation,

> I feel like church and Christianity is known for who we don't like, and the bad things that we make people feel and churches grabbing onto that and making it the defining thing about themselves that is different to other churches, I feel like it's very dangerous . . . We seem to be going down that path of, 'we're affirming, we are not affirming' and that's characteristic of the church. I guess I think it is necessary now, in this current time today.[265]

On the nature of the church, another felt that the purpose of a local gathering should be more focused on, 'relationship between those

---

[264] Focus Group Transcript.
[265] Focus Group Transcript.

who want to truly love the Lord,'[266] suggesting more of an overlap between the two expressions of covenant relationship.

John Claydon concludes that 'although Baptist churches are enclave communities with the corporate personality of the individualist, their relational values provide an opportunity to encourage informal relationships and collaboration for the sake of common endeavour and mutual support.'[267] This interpersonal value was expressed by participants through their mutual desire for unity, although contributors additionally expressed an acceptance that the nature of relationships at a trans-local level would likely vary from those developed within their place of membership, with one person reflecting, 'you can't be friends with everyone in every way . . .'[268] Group members vocalised a willingness to meet in a social context, outside of the focus group setting, with the anticipation that it would encourage reflexivity across differing churches, with another continuing, 'if there was an active thing, a Baptist social, then it would allow people to learn from each other. I think that's the point.'[269] Association has the potential to counter the negative consequences of homogeneity by encouraging organic social interaction between member churches. These interactions, which again would not result in uniformity of view, may enable members from differing

---

[266] Focus Group Transcript.

[267] John Claydon, *Bound Together in the Liberty of Christ: Renewing Baptist Collaboration in Mission.* (University of Durham, PhD, 2013), 197.

[268] Focus Group Transcript.

[269] Focus Group Transcript.

contexts to explore theology voluntarily while maintaining individual church membership in a safe environment.

Beyond this, we have an opportunity to practice congregational leadership since the contemporary question about equal marriage challenges the nature of the authority of the church. A hierarchy of expectation seems to be reflected throughout several of the voices speaking into this subject, one example being the practice of local churches, 35% of which have adopted theologies of marriage shaped primarily by the views of leadership teams rather than the entirety of the church body. On these distinctions, one group member stated, 'the priesthood of all believers doesn't make that distinction between the priests and the laity, as it were.'[270] A return to Paul's writings (Gal 3.28) does not support this elevation of some voices at the expense of others; rather, there is a clear emphasis on the requirement of the contemporary church to listen to those who have been overlooked in the past. Embracing our Baptist identity in local contexts could create opportunities to start conversations 'without consequence.' This is in the sense that open dialogue is created in a safe environment, which is not necessarily succeeded by a church vote. Conversation in this instance was possible because participants did not feel threatened by the outcome of the discussions, and while this may not be suitable for all churches, ongoing dialogue within the church (in its entirety) is a necessity moving forward. Whilst, long term, churches must offer an outline of their position in order for believers to be able to make informed choices about

---

[270] Focus Group Transcript.

membership within that setting, as a starting point within the current climate, initial conversations are an improvement from the silence that dominates. Forming theologies as whole church communities, in association (where association is characterised by genuine depth of relationship) with other Baptist faith groups, enables us to collectively hear what God might be communicating to our movement and learn from each other in a manner that is encouraged by the freedom that is part of the basis of our Union, outworking the priesthood of all believers and creating safe spaces for voices that might be entirely new to us. This is what it means to live out our Baptist identity in the present day.

Interestingly, the methods of addressing the current challenges faced by Baptists are not new to us. Many would likely already agree with the principles of covenant, association, and conversation. In actuality, they are much harder to live out, particularly in a context within which there has been an absence of healthy conversation, but this does not have to be the continued trajectory of the Baptist movement. During this process of reflection, nobody changed their theology of marriage. Participants reflected that the invitation to share their own views, rather than attempt to change those of others, offered a sense of humility and reassurance. Interactions with those holding differing views, in this case, did not merely foster toleration among the group but created an experience in which the fruits of the Spirit could be observed:

> It's actually something really humbling about accepting someone, and actually you don't have to change anyone

145

else's mind... that's quite a humbling experience because when you accept that you're no longer on the attack, as such. I'm here to present my beliefs and my opinions and actually, if I know that the other people in the room are not here to change my idea, I don't have to go on the defense either. I can just say what I believe and not try and change anyone else and not have anyone else try and change me.[271]

---

[271] Focus Group Transcript.

6   Welsh Baptist Worship: Now and Then - A Hope of Retrieval?

Tomos Roberts-Young

There is hardly a Christian tradition whose worship is not imbued with the sound of God's children singing.[272] This is no less true of the Baptist tradition in west Wales, whose tradition has been shaped by a form of worship known as *Canu Pwnc* (Singing the Subject), where congregants would sing portions of Scripture in a *Gymanfa Bwnc* (a worship service dedicated to the singing and expounding of the text). However, in recent years, there has been a startling decline in the practice by ordinary Welsh speaking Baptist congregations, with a marked reduction in the number of active participants. Indeed, *Canu Pwnc* runs the risk of being wholly displaced in Welsh Baptist churches by Contemporary Christian Music (CCM). The chapter aims to bridge the gap between CCM and *Canu Pwnc* and, in doing so, will demonstrate its relevance to a church culture which often discards such traditions in favour of CCM. Firstly, I will trace and contextualise the historical roots of *Canu Pwnc*. Secondly, I will draw attention to the displacement of *Canu Pwnc* by CCM. While I concede that CCM has its place within contemporary Welsh Baptist culture, it also occludes different expressions of worship from being explored in the contemporary church. Finally, the chapter will conclude by arguing that while *Canu Pwnc* should not be

---

[272] The Religious Society of Friends is an obvious exception to this.

mimicked for the sake of history, the practice should be retrieved as a spiritual exercise that roots the church in her ongoing history.[273]

Canu Pwnc: A Living History

Helen Barlow writes, 'The innate musicality of the Welsh may be a dubious proposition, but the fundamental link between Welsh musical culture and religion is an important and real one.'[274] This is not to say that singing the Scriptures is a distinctively Welsh practice. As Michael Legaspi has pointed out, Scripture is itself a body of literature comprising the liturgy of Ancient Israel that was used for singing and worshipping God.[275] Indeed, the nascent

---

[273] There is scant literature surrounding *Canu Pwnc*, both academic and popular level. Thus, to better understand the practice of *Canu Pwnc* it has been necessary to conduct interviews with those who have engaged with, and participated in, the practice. The first section will heavily rely on interviews conducted by those who have engaged with and practiced *Canu Pwnc* from a number of Baptistic churches. The descriptions of the memories each person has of *Canu Pwnc* vary and thus as each voice contributes, we will be able to better understand what happens when one participates in a *Gymanfa Bwnc*. The following questions were asked to each interviewee: 1) What are your memories of *Canu Pwnc*? 2) Can you describe a *Gymanfa Bwnc*? 3) How important was it for your faith in childhood and if so, why was it important? 4) How has Canu Pwnc impacted on your spiritual life? 5) Did it help you to develop your understanding of God, the Bible, and/or theology? 6) How do you see the future of *Canu Pwnc* as a means of worship?

[274] Helen Barlow, 'Praise the Lord! We are a musical nation': the Welsh working classes and religious singing.' *Nineteenth-Century Music Review* 17:3 (December 2020): 445-72.

[275] Michael Legaspi, *The Death of Scripture and the Rise of Biblical Studies*

church incorporated the Scriptures of the Hebrew Bible into their worship before the development of a New Testament canon. With this, each local context has responded to Scripture in its own unique way. Welsh Baptists have done this through their own distinct way of singing *Canu Pwnc*. In this section, I trace the origins of the practice of *Canu Pwnc* before describing a service.

Canu Pwnc has never been practised throughout the whole of Wales. Rather, in the same way as Gaelic Psalm singing is unique to the Hebrides, *Canu Pwnc*'s origins and continued practice is particular to south-west Wales, particularly the counties of Carmarthenshire and Pembrokeshire. In these areas, such a tradition has a long history. As early as 1668, Welsh Baptist churches had been established in south-west Wales in Rhydwilym, Pembrokeshire, during a period of religious persecution which prohibited a gathering for worship by religious sects other than the established parish churches: the Church of England. One of the respondents to my interviews, who became the minister of the Baptist church in Rhydwilym, writes that 'among the early practices of the church at Rhydwilym was the *"Gymanfa Bwnc"*.'[276] It was still practised until at least 2019 Rhydwilym, with around a dozen present worshipping.[277] Of course, the effects of the Covid-19 pandemic on church life across Wales have affected this, and it remains to be seen if this practice,

---

(Oxford: Oxford University Press, 2011).

[276] Interviewee 1, Interview, Conducted by Tomos Roberts-Young (TRY).

[277] Interviewee 5, Interview, Conducted by TRY.

which has been ongoing for over 300 years in Rhydwilym, will survive.

A *Gymanfa Bwnc* is a worship service that would occur once a year 'in one of the chapels and the congregations of the other chapels would join the host church, with a change of location every year.'[278] This would be on the *Llungwyn* (Whit Monday), the Monday after Whitsun. In the weeks leading up to the *Gymanfa Bwnc*, between Easter and Pentecost, 'a passage of scripture was chosen by the Minister and then over a few weeks (4 perhaps) a midweek meeting was held to go over the Pwnc.'[279] One interviewee writes that 'the *Pwnc* was an opportunity to focus on one piece of scripture and not a typical Sunday School lesson that would look less in-depth for a piece of Scripture.'[280] Thus, it was a period of particularly intense devotion to studying the Scriptures. Accompanying the meeting of going over the Pwnc, would be an *Ysgol Gân* (Singing School) to practice singing the Pwnc.[281] The importance of such events for the communities of south-west Wales should not be underestimated, with one interviewee remembering that it was an occasion for new clothes, an occurrence saved only for special occasions in such poor Welsh communities.[282]

---

[278] Interviewee 2, Interview, Conducted by TRY.
[279] Interviewee 3, Interview, Conducted by TRY.
[280] Interviewee 4, Interview, Conducted by TRY.
[281] Interviewee 4, Interview, Conducted by TRY.
[282] Interviewee 6, Interview, Conducted by TRY.

Although called the singing of the subject, the interviewees emphasised that it was more of using your voice to 'chant the passage in a unique way.'[283] One noted that 'the chapter would be relatively long and divided into sections. Everyone starts [singing] together and then parts for the men and women separately with everyone coming together to finish.'[284] One writes that 'The chant echoed the singing in plainsong which was reminiscent of monastic music. Each chapel had a particular and peculiar chant.'[285] Thus they named their chant after their chapel. One interviewee tried to explain how it might sound: 'The women would pitch the top SOH and the men the DOH below.'[286] However, such descriptions cannot adequately capture the nature of *Canu Pwnc*. As one noted, 'The sound is quite unique and difficult to explain in writing. The "Canu Pwnc" must be heard in order to appreciate its unique sound.'[287] Despite the practice only occurring within a small area in Wales, much variation was to be found. One interviewee wrote, 'The practice varied from area to area. For example, our Pwnc chanting was reasonably of a monotone nature, whereas other areas had a different intonation, more exciting, e.g. [the] First syllable was extended, and the penultimate syllable was lowered in tone.'[288] All of this suggests that despite local to south-west Wales, it was not a monolithic

---

[283] Interviewee 2, Interview, Conducted by TRY.

[284] Interviewee 4, Interview, Conducted by TRY.

[285] Interviewee 1, Interview, Conducted by TRY.

[286] Interviewee 1, Interview, Conducted by TRY.

[287] Interviewee 1, Interview, Conducted by TRY.

[288] Interviewee 3, Interview, Conducted by TRY.

tradition, and each area gave rise to their own particular form of worship.

The *Gymanfa Bwnc* is not limited to the singing. Following the singing, or chanting, of the passage, 'the Scripture would be discussed.' This is a response to the *Canu Pwnc*, which is called *Holi Pwnc* (asking, or questioning the subject). The *Holi* would then be led by the '*Holwr*' (one who asks), usually the minister of the hosting church. Thus, together *Canu Pwnc* and *Holi Pwnc* form a *Gymanfa Bwnc*. Indeed, the freedom given in a *Gymanfa Bwnc* was not seen during normal Sunday services. As one interviewee answered, 'any individual was free to answer from [their] seat.'[289] However, the limits of these freedoms seem to be varied between congregations. One interviewee writes that 'questions were asked by the leader, usually the resident minister, and members of the congregation answered, usually the deacons.' Yet, even if the voices were limited to the deacons, which was more than what most were used to during the Sunday service. As one interviewee noted: 'As a child I would just listen and was enthralled by the whole procedure. One thing that was strange was hearing voices of people in the chapel. Usually, only two voices would ever be heard speaking in chapel, the minister, and the announcer. So it was strange to hear the voices of other people taking part in the service.'[290] The impact of this, as one interviewee wrote, is that 'The Pwnc provided an opportunity…to learn passages of Scripture by heart and enabled verses of

---

[289] Interviewee 2, Interview, Conducted by TRY.
[290] Interviewee 3, Interview, Conducted by TRY.

Scripture once remembered to be recalled to mind and become a basis for conviction and belief.'[291] Another writes 'The tradition has grown on me and I relish any opportunity to engage in spiritual and biblical discussion. It opens my mind and allows me to see the Word in a different light.'[292]

This is far from a picture of a peaceful church coming together to learn lines by rote - even if practising to perfect the *Pwnc* was an important part of the preparations. According to some interviewees, the period of *Holi Pwnc* could be a time of fervent debate. As one interviewee writes, 'sometimes heated debate ensued. So the discussion of the gallery and the minister in the pulpit can be entertaining and quite fiery at times!'[293] This is further attested as another writes that 'there would be a lively interchange of opinions and ideas.'[294] This, however, evidently varied from congregation to congregation - as one answered, 'there were no "surprises" in the questions in the Gymanfa Bwnc, nothing to rock the spiritual boat!'[295]

It is worth concluding our delineation of how a *Canu Pwnc* functions in the context of a *Gymanfa Bwnc* by noting that each

---

[291] Interviewee 1, Interview, Conducted by TRY.

[292] Interviewee 5, Interview, Conducted by TRY.

[293] Interviewee 4, Interview, Conducted by TRY.

[294] Interviewee 2, Interview, Conducted by TRY.

[295] The interviewee further notes. 'In order to avoid too much debate or arguments, some ministers would provide all the questions and answers on paper in advance so that someone could give the right answer.' Interviewee 3, Interview, Conducted by TRY.

of these respondents expressed great doubt about its future. Such responses ranged from 'I do not see a future for Canu Pwnc' to a slightly more hopeful 'it might be possible to re-introduce *Canu Pwnc.*'[296] But 'as with everything else, the numbers are dwindling.'[297] We will return to these concerns in the final section of this chapter. Prior to that, we must address one of the greatest challenges facing the future of *Canu Pwnc*: Contemporary Christian Music.

Competing Cultures: Canu Pwnc and the Challenge of Contemporary Christian Music

For a number of historical and cultural reasons, not least the rise of non-conformity, singing the Scriptures is not as prevalent today as it once was.[298] Inspired, perhaps, by such sentiments as '*Why Should the Devil Have all the Good Music,*' an increasing growth in the use of more popular musical styles has been witnessed in churches. While there are clear benefits to the growth of CCM, the clear side-effect is the displacement of older forms of worship – with the growth of CCM coinciding with the demise of *Canu Pwnc*. This section will examine this displacement by focusing on

---

[296] Interviewee 3 and 2, Interview, Conducted by TRY.

[297] Interviewee 5, Interview, Conducted by TRY.

[298] Ian Bradley, 'Nonconformist Hymnody' in *T&T Clark Companion to Nonconformity* edited by Robert Pope (London: T&T Clark: 2016), 235-246. Cf. For a brief history of the Psalms on the British Isles before the rise of non-conformity, see Timothy Duguid, *Metrical Psalms in Print and Practice, St Andrews Studies in Reformation History* (New York, US: Routledge, 2016), 1-48.

two main points. Firstly, it will draw attention to a number of problems that CCM might have in a Welsh Baptistic context and argue, secondly, that these forms need not be in a competitive relationship to one another but rather that each has its place in the contemporary church.

CCM should be seen as 'a blend of rock and pop with religious lyrics.'[299] Mark Allen Powell expands on this and writes that 'artists in the Christian rock scene have a tendency to copy the styles of successful mainstream performers in order to provide godly alternatives to whatever is popular at the time.'[300] This is part of evangelicalism's 'perpetual reinvention of old-time religion' that is as true in America as it is in Wales.[301] What distinguishes the Welsh context from its Anglo-American counterpart is that in Wales, the majority of the new songs that are introduced to Welsh speaking churches in Wales are translations of English CCM songs. This can be seen on *Gobaith Cymru* (Wales' Hope), a website run by *Cyngor Ysgolion Sul* (Sunday Schools Council), which compiles different worship songs into

---

[299] Courtney Tepera, 'Created to Worship: The Practice of Devotional Listening and Christian Contemporary Music', *Artistic Theologian* 6 (2018): 33-49.

[300] Mark Allen Powell, 'Jesus climbs the charts: the business of contemporary Christian music', *The Christian Century*, 119.26 (Dec 18 - 31 2002): 20-26.

[301] Kate Bowler and Wen Reagan, 'Bigger, better, louder: the prosperity gospel's impact on contemporary Christian worship, *Religion and American Culture* 24.2 (Sumer 2014): 186-230. See also Bradley, 'Nonconformist Hymnody'.

three categories - Modern Translations (481), Original Songs (73), and Traditional Hymns (862).[302] As the figures show, there are over six times as many translations from English as original compositions of Welsh CCM. Moreover, even if there are some original Welsh language songs, with the influence of modern translations on Welsh baptistic culture, one cannot escape the fact that much of the form and content of these original songs will necessarily have mirrored their Anglo-American counterparts.

This is not to say that there are no benefits to CCM in the Welsh speaking church. Addressing a different cultural context, Courtney Tepera, summarises some of the positive effects of CCM on people's lives, writing that by 'intentionally imbuing [her respondents] daily lives with religious music, they create an atmosphere that reinforces their Christian identities by strengthening their faith and calming their emotions.'[303] Moreover, although heavily critical of CCM, Fiona Parascandalo writes 'the musical advancement that attracts new listeners and satisfies the musical wants of the community also operates to further the evangelical objective of conversion since the songs contain the values which have always been present in the Christian faith.'[304] Such ideas are prevalent within the evangelical

---

[302] Cyngor Ysgolion Sul, *Gobaith Cymru*, (accessed 12/07/2022), http://www.gobaith.cymru/category/math-o-gan/traddodiadol/

[303] Tepera, 'Created to Worship: The Practice of Devotional Listening and Christian Contemporary Music', *Artistic Theologian 6* (2018): 49.

[304] Fiona Parascandalo, 'Thou Shalt Get thy Praise On!: Analysis on the Conversion and Community Maintenance Powers of Contemporary Christian Music', *Journal of Religion and Popular Culture* 25.2 (Summer 2013): 205-

wing of the Baptist tradition in Wales and may be seen by some as an important facet of British Baptist identity which calls on Baptists to 'bear personal witness to the Gospel of Jesus Christ, and to take part in the evangelisation of the world.'[305] Faced with a sharp decline in church attendance, many churches seem to have incorporated CCM in an attempt to increase the relevancy and accessibility of worship by incorporating modern popular forms of music familiar to them in their daily lives.

Despite such positive effects, the increasing incorporation of CCM in contemporary Baptist churches comes at a cost – both within the specific context of Welsh culture and with regards to more general problems. A comparison can be made between the rise of translating CCM songs into Welsh and the story of Bishop Colenso as he embarked on 'one of the most important odysseys of a missionary bishop in the history of the Christian church' from England to South Africa, set out by Willie James Jennings in his work *The Christian Imagination*.[306] This story provides some insights with regards to the dangers for Welsh culture being assimilated with Anglo-American culture. Jennings describes the story of Bishop Colenso, an Anglican shaped by the Church of

---

16.

[305] This is the third heading of the Baptist Union of Great Britain and *Undeb Bedyddwyr Cymru*/Baptist Union of Wales' Y *Datganiad o Egwyddor/Declaration of Principles*. In Welsh: Dyletswydd pob disgybl yw tystio'n bersonol i Efengyl Iesu Grist ac i gymryd rhan mewn efengyleiddio'r byd.

[306] Willie James Jennings, *The Christian Imagination*, (New Haven, CT: Yale University Press, 2010), 119.

England, as he embarks on a journey from England to South Africa.[307] Here, we can see analogies between him arriving in South Africa from England and his role in translating Christian texts from the dominant language (the English language) to a minority language (the Zulu language) and Welsh speakers translating English songs into the Welsh language. The difference between the two stories is who is doing the translating - in our case, it is the practitioners of the minority language themselves who are doing the translating. In this work, Jennings notes that despite Bishop Colenso's important work that ultimately should be celebrated, he did this 'under the canopy of preparing proper colonial subjects.'[308] Thus, Colenso's Christianity ended as a form of universalism that 'undermines all forms of identity except that of the colonialist.'[309] Similarly, we see that CCM's incorporation into Welsh speaking Baptistic churches undermines the particular context in which *Canu Pwnc* was developed.

Suren Pillay writes that for Africa 'colonial assimilation sought to refashion the colonised subject in the image of European man in consciousness, comportment, conduct, and aesthetics.'[310] We see that through CCM, Welsh speaking Baptists are in danger of being assimilated into the image of an Anglo-American person, taken away from their original worship context, and losing any sense of

---

[307] Jennings, *The Christian Imagination*, 119.

[308] Jennings, *The Christian Imagination*, 132.

[309] Jennings, *The Christian Imagination*, 145.

[310] Suren Pillay, 'The Problem of Colonialism: Assimilation, Difference, and Decolonial Theory in Africa', *Critical Times* 4.3 (2021): 389–416.

the identities that make up our shared sense of Welshness.[311] The danger of being assimilated into a dominant culture cannot be overstated. Although, as with the Bible being translated into the Zulu language, there are some benefits to the translating, Welsh language translators must be careful, however, that they understand the overarching dangers that exist to minority cultures from dominant cultures; especially as the minority culture faces cultural and linguistic eradication. Despite such dangers, translating CCM into Welsh has become a necessary aspect of contemporary Welsh baptistic life. We simply do not have the same resources to produce as many new songs or compositions. Moreover, one cannot deny the benefits of such translations. In Welsh language Christian conferences across Wales, hundreds of people will attest to benefitting from hearing contemporary worship music that to which they can relate. This comes with a glaring warning from Jennings: 'If translation is necessary for Christian theology, it is also dangerous.'[312]

All too often older and newer forms of worship are pitted against each other, as if one had to choose their favourite form. The Baptist church has always been a reforming church. Drawing on this rich history of Baptist theology, one can expect to hear CCM in Baptist churches' worship services, because of the evangelistic

---

[311] Two points are to be made here. First, this chapter does not seek to negate or undermine the reality that Wales had deep connections to imperialism and transatlantic slavery. Second, I emphasise plural to remind myself and the reader that *Canu Pwnc* should not be seen as essential to Welshness but as one particular part of a tapestry of imaginative ways to be Welsh.

[312] Jennings, *The Christian Imagination*, 161.

impulse that is inherent in many Baptistic theologies. Nevertheless, by drawing on the same history, we see the importance and often continued importance of older styles of worship. Whatever the hitherto unexplored reason as to why Wales has succumbed to the allure of CCM (aside from the obvious answer of neoliberal market forces), there is hope that Welsh speaking Baptists might rethink the role of worship. In a recent work, Stephen Woodhams writes that 'What . . . marks Wales and the Welsh, was a capacity to create a culture both in the sense of a way of life and as creative expression. The two modes intertwined in hymn singing, band playing, acting, playing ball, or building temples that became chapels, miners institute and libraries.'[313] In what ways will Welsh speaking Baptists create culture anew in the 21st Century? The next section seeks to ask how might Baptists embody this lived tradition and reimagine *Canu Pwnc* in the contemporary world?

A Living Hope: Retrieving the Past to Make Sense of the Present

As evinced in the last section, a number of issues are identified with the appropriation of CCM into Welsh speaking culture, even if one does concede that it is an important, or inescapable, part of contemporary baptistic culture in Wales. Thus, if Baptistic churches want *Canu Pwnc* to be retrieved from its current decline, one must build a case as to why the past might be able to expand our experiences of the Christian experience in the present and

---

[313] Stephen Woohams, 'A Longer History' in *Raymond Williams: Wales to The World* edited by Stephen Woodhams (Cardigan, Wales, 2021), 16-17.

future. Elsewhere on the British Isles, Gaelic Psalm singing is experiencing widespread attention. Moreover, *Plygain*, singing that occurs during Advent and *Gŵyl Fair y Canhwyllau* (Mary's Festival of the Candles or Candlemas), has received much attention in recent years in Wales.[314] This chapter is written with the conviction that *Canu Pwnc* too has a future in the midst of these other emerging retrievals of traditional folk worship. For contemporary research, the possibilities of understanding *Canu Pwnc* through a number of intersectionalities abound - not only in the church but for those who wish to explore the role that it has had in the lives of west-Wales' population. In this section, I will limit myself to those who specifically relate to Baptistic experiences of the Christian faith to argue that *Canu Pwnc* does have a role to play in the future of Baptist churches in Wales.

Describing the situation in the Baptist Unions of Great Britain and Scotland, Stephen Holmes writes that 'Baptists are, at least historically, a people defined by the Bible.' He further argues, commenting on the general state of Baptists' commitment to the Scriptures, that 'my suspicion and observation…is that in most Baptist services, Scripture will be confined to one, often very brief, passage read immediately before the sermon.'[315] We saw, above, that in certain Welsh Baptistic contexts, this was simply

---

[314] Specifically, through the research of Rhiannon Ifans. Here is a blog by Ifans which has an example of Plygain: https://blog.library.wales/plygain/ (accessed 12/07/2022)

[315] Stephen R. Holmes, 'Baptists and the Bible', *Baptist Quarterly* 43:7 (2010): 410-427.

not the case during the period between in the weeks leading up to Whitsun. Incorporating *Canu Pwnc* into the yearly pattern of the church has the possibility of bringing the spirit of Acts 8: 26-40 into the worship of the church where Peter asks, 'Do you understand what you are reading?' and the Eunuch replies: 'How can I unless someone explains it to me?' Rather than limiting our use of Scripture to in sung worship and to singing and reflecting on translated modern songs, with its manifold problems, singing *Canu Pwnc* moves the Baptist churches back to what they're most known for — the Bible. As one respondent answered 'it would be a good thing for congregations, including youngsters, to study Scripture together and maybe learn verses, as learning by heart . . . is not common in these modern times.'[316] This has the two-fold advantage of bringing Baptists back to their historical roots as people defined by the Bible and specifically bringing Welsh Baptists back to a form of worship that is rooted in their own particular history.[317]

One of the respondents was not hopeful of the future of *Canu Pwnc* but persisted that 'It is a tradition that *must* be upheld, and is looked upon as an important part of the church calendar.' (Emphasis added).[318] Part of the lasting appeal of *Canu Pwnc* to the respondents was the effect that it had on their spiritual lives.

---

[316] Interviewee 2, Interview, Conducted by TRY.

[317] One interviewee noted that with the demise of the Sunday school, the Gymanfa Bwnc was the only opportunity to study the Scriptures in depth in their church. Interviewee 5, Interview, Conducted by TRY.

[318] Interviewee 5, Interview, Conducted by TRY.

162

As one interviewee wrote, 'I definitely feel that *Canu Pwnc* solidifies the meaning of the gospel words in the mind and heart.'[319] The spiritual effects of worship are a frequently discussed topic by God's people. The Hebrew Bible tells of David and Saul, that 'whenever the harmful spirit from God was upon Saul, David took the lyre and played it with his hand. So, Saul was refreshed and was well, and the harmful spirit departed from him' (1 Samuel 16:23). In the history of the church, John Chrystostom writes that 'With chanting the air becomes saintly . . . The mind listens to the voice, and it changes; the melody enters and impiety is changed, escaping the passions of greed.'[320] Indeed, Welsh Baptist would do well to heed John Chrystostom's words and rediscover the beauty of the spiritual effects of Scriptures as part of the ongoing spiritual formation of the church as the church is gathered by the triune God to worship.

Canu Pwnc has a deep impact on not only the theological education of the interviewees but also has had a lasting impact on their spiritual lives. Despite the fact that the *Gymanfa Bwnc* is dwindling, evinced from the answers of the interviewees is the way in which *Canu Pwnc* affected their relationship with God. If Welsh speaking Baptist churches are to take seriously the role of caring for the souls of those of all ages, one must not run away with the idea that old practices have no space for the continued spiritual edification of the church. As one contemporary writer

---

[319] Interviewee 6, Interview, Conducted by TRY.

[320] St John Chrysostom. Homily after the earthquake, *Patrologia Graeca* 50, 714.

says, 'another important source of meaning and hope is found in spiritual traditions common to most religions, including liturgy, worship, and prayer. It seems that when depression leads people to struggle intellectually with their faith, the elements of ritual, symbol and habit associated with these traditions are able to "carry a person through" their worst moments.'[321] On the other hand, contemporary music's effect on culture and the mind has not received the same praise.[322]

This desire to keep the tradition, however, cannot be done without reform. The Scriptures remind us of the faith that was once for all time handed down to the saints (see Jude 3). Bringing Baptists back to their tradition does not mean simply replicating it. As we saw above, one of the respondents writes that the 'questions were asked by the leader, usually the resident minister and members of the congregation answered, *usually the deacons*' (emphasis added).[323] Another responded saying that 'One might be critical of this practice happening in a Baptist church.' Of course, many Baptists retain an understanding of a specific calling to church leadership, however, that might look across different Baptist traditions.[324] However, as Holmes argues, 'the mind of Christ is

---

[321] Sushama Bhosale, 'Impact of Spirituality on Mental Health', *International Journal of Current Research* 7:5 (2015).

[322] See for example Theodore Adorno, 'On the Fetish Character' in *The Culture Industry: Selected Essays on Mass Culture* edited by J. M. Bernstein (London: Routledge, 1991), 34-35.

[323] Interviewee 3, Interview, Conducted by TRY.

[324] See especially *The Second London Baptist Confession of Faith* (1677) which makes a distinction between the leaders and members, writing that 'a

given by the Spirit to the gathered people within the local church. On a Baptist view, therefore, authority rests in Christ alone, but because Christ's will is discerned in the church meeting, authority derivatively rests with *all* the members of the church corporately' (emphasis added).[325] Moreover, evidently from all of the respondents *Canu Pwnc* was an important formative part of their theological education. Under this understanding, the practice of answering the minister's questions during the period of *Holi'r Pwnc* might encourage a broader number of congregants to participate in answering questions on the sung text. This, in turn, will hopefully encourage the congregation to expand on their understanding and interpretations of Scripture within their particular congregation, as opposed to the minister being the only one expounding the text.

Another example of reforming the tradition might be better incorporation of younger people into *Gymanfa Pwnc*. This is especially true for a Baptist tradition since, as Holmes writes, as a church tradition which does not baptise children 'a Baptist church is always very visibly one generation away from extinction.' The interviewees provided contrasting answers with regard to the role of children in a *Gymanfa Pwnc*. One answered

---

particular church, gathered and completely Organized, according to the mind of Christ, consists of Officers and Members . . . for the peculiar Administration of Ordinances, and Execution of Power, or Duty, which he entrusts them with, or calls them to, to be continued to the end of the world, are Bishops or Elders and Deacons', *Baptist Confessions of Faith* edited by William L. Lumpkin and Bill J. Leonard (2nd Rev. Ed.; Valley Forge, PA: Judson Press, 2011), 286

[325] Stephen Holmes, *Baptist Theology* (London: T & T Clark, 2012), 111.

that they had 'no early memories of *Canu Pwnc*, as children were not involved during my childhood.'[326] Rather, they continue, 'my father and other adult members of the church where I grew up would stay in the chapel after the evening service to prepare for the *Gymanfa Bwnc*.' Whilst others answered that 'The *Pwnc* provided an opportunity for children as well as Adults to learn passages of Scripture by heart,' and 'As a child I would just listen and was enthralled by the whole procedure.'[327] Despite the fact that there are contrasting answers, it is obvious that for the majority of the interviewees, there was a separation between the adults and the children.

Another aspect is the existence of the Welsh language, which has declined dramatically over the past two centuries. Its continued existence is a matter of justice. Questions, however, must be raised as to whether contemporary Baptist churches can call on this injustice to be overturned by singing CCM songs. In a recent article, Brenda Eatman Aghahowa, whose work focuses on the Black church, argues that 'contemporary worship often does quite a poor job of asking people to think deeply about major societal issues outside of their own narrow circumstances. It does not help them to think about how the Bible speaks to those issues or about the ways they might take action to address them.'[328] This essay

---

[326] Interviewee 2, Interview, Conducted by TRY.

[327] Interviewee 3, Interview, Conducted by TRY.

[328] Brenda Eatman Aghahowa, 'The Need for Milk and Meat in Contemporary Christian Worship Part Two: Preaching More than "Hold out until My Change Come"', *Liturgy* 36.1 (Jan-Mar 2021): 42-48.

does not claim that *Canu Pwnc* necessarily brings forth actions of justice in the church any more than CCM does. The evidence is certainly lacking. Nevertheless, with the abundance of references to justice in the Scriptures, the possibility of worshipping becoming a cry against injustices perpetuated towards (or by) Welsh speaking communities as part of the Baptist church's regular worship. From Owain Glyndwr's war of rebellion against the Kingdom of England to the Tonypandy riots (1910-11), ending with Churchill sending troops to south Wales; the cry — '*O Arglwydd, dyma Gamwedd* — Oh Lord, This is an Injustice' — has been cried out in Wales for centuries.[329] *Canu Pwnc*, with its focus on the Scriptures, allows for a possibility of an ongoing voice for Baptists to reflect on injustices in Wales, a country whose identities has been neglected by the British government for centuries and shaped by its cries of injustices.[330]

This should be accompanied by encouraging active work of justice in the church to redress the fact that evidence of singing of

---

[329] The (apparent) last words of Dic Penderyn (1808-1831) who died at 23. Penderyn was a Welsh labourer and coal miner who took part in the Merthyr Rising in 1831.

[330] Perhaps the most striking example of injustices perpetuated by the British state that lingers in the popular mind is the flooding of a rural community in north Wales, Capel Celyn, to provide water for Liverpool. This was despite opposition from 35 of the 36 sitting Welsh MPs in Westminster. 'Everyone deplores the fact that in the interests of progress some people must suffer…But that is progress,' were the words of the sitting MP for Liverpool, Bessie Braddock. See https://www.theguardian.com/uk/2001/jan/27/davidward.

or actions of justice was absent in the interviews conducted. This is of deep importance since, as Juan José Barreda Toscano writes, 'Addressing the subject of justice without being involved in the work of justice short-circuits the epistemological possibility of understanding the divine revelation.'[331] Moreover, music is not theologically neutral nor is it soteriologically neutral. As Christoph Schwöbel writes 'it is one of the greatest capacities of music that it can express both, the distortion of communicative relations, the cry for liberation and the yearning and the anticipatory joy of the overcoming of distortions.'[332] Thus, as much as *Canu Pwnc* can contribute to the ongoing cry for liberation, it should also linger on the joys as Welsh Baptistic churches anticipate a future in Wales where justice triumphs over evil. The examples given in this section as to why *Canu Pwnc* should constitute a greater part of Welsh language Baptistic churches are merely the beginning of a conversation that I hope has far wider implications. The hope is that future work will on this topic will encourage a deeper engagement with a tradition that is not yet dead.

---

[331] Juan José Barreda Toscano, Bible Study in Latin America, *Journal of Latin American Theology* 10:2 (2015): 88.

[332] Christoph Schwöbel, 'Mutual resonances: remarks on the relationship between music and theology', *International Journal for the Study of the Christian Church* 20:1 (2020): 8-22.

Conclusion

This chapter has sought to bring to light a dying tradition that was once prevalent among Welsh baptistic churches in Carmarthenshire and Pembrokeshire. In the contemporary world, resisting Anglo-American culture is near impossible, and CCM is here in the church to stay. This should not, however, mean that we should forget the saints that came before whose tradition of singing the Scriptures is intertwined with their and our language and culture. The recent revival of various Christian folk traditions across the UK, including Wales, gives the Baptist church in Wales a hope that, likewise, a greater awareness might come to *Canu Pwnc*. This is as true of English folk cultures as it is of Celtic folk traditions. As much as the existence of various worship styles in the UK is of pressing concern for Welsh and Gaelic traditions, it is also should be a concern for English speakers. They, too, would do well to engage with the panoply of traditional and emerging traditions of worship that run counter-culturally to CCM and explore the ways in which the dominant popular culture has sought to undermine English folk traditions. This comes with a warning in itself. One interviewee wrote that, 'I would be delighted to go back to that time again.'[333] Baptist churches who wish to reengage with the tradition must not fetishise it. Rather, they should seek to engage critically with it and proceed in a way that expands on the current tradition in constructive ways that seek to build the kingdom of God in Welsh speaking baptistic

---

[333] Interviewee 6, Interview, Conducted by TRY.

churches. With this in mind, I am confident that there is a hope for the retrieval of *Canu Pwnc*.

7 Dissent, De-colonisation and the De-Churched

Eleasah P. Louis

In the last few years, I have wondered if it is possible to rediscover Christianity, particularly if you have been born into the fold and spent every year of your life in the church, 'doing church.' I had spent many enthusiastic late teenage years wanting to serve the church in any way I could, but as is often the case, when churches transition, it becomes an opportunity for individuals to ask deep and meaningful questions.

During a particular church transition, where my pastor of nearly forty years was retiring, and the church's first Black minister was to step into the senior role, I, for the first time, began to see the mechanics of Baptist-ness at work. I had understood that a believer's baptism was a core theological distinction but was less articulate in the other Baptist practices such as congregationalist church government, the process for the appointment of ministers, the free-church principle, the role of the broader Associations and Union (should the church choose to participate) and its historical rooting in radical dissent or as '*dissenters*.' Looking back, I can see how my Baptist church engaged with those mechanisms, but at the time, I could not connect them to the context from which this *modus operandi* was birthed. European radical dissenters were asking *could they rediscover a Christianity rooted back in*

Scripture, not competing with spurious Roman Catholic Tradition? In a similar breath, many Black people in Britain are asking — *can we rediscover the religion of the Biblical Messiah despite centuries of European Christianisation?*

My day-to-day research is concerned with the phenomena of Black Bible religions in Britain, such as the Rastafari, The Nation of Islam, The Holy Qubtic Church and the Black Hebrew Israelites — particularly their ongoing influence in the twenty-first century. These religions, sometimes termed 'Black Mystery Cults'[334] in Black Urban Apologetic circles, may be considered fringe, controversial, and to some dangerous — yet when considering the phenomena historically and methodologically, there are some similarities to the birth of protestants — they too are dissenters.

Therefore, in this chapter, I am drawing my insights as a researcher on decolonisation, Black religions in Britain, and theology and as a conservative evangelical (Baptist) Christian to reflect on Baptist identity and to consider how the bedfellows — 'dissent' and 'decolonisation' — naturally lead to anti-racism, despite the divides and tensions within our Baptist community on this topic.

Andy Goodliff has suggested that being Baptist is about participating in a conversation about what it means to be a

---

[334] Eric Mason, *Woke Church: An Urgent Call for Christians in America to Confront Racism and Injustice* (Chicago: Moody Publishers, 2018).

172

Baptist.[335] When I read this, I thought of the social reflexivity that is part of the nature of 'being Baptist': being moved, shaken, and responding to the evolution of the wider society and considering how it shapes our presence, local ministry, and activism as Baptists in Britain.

I have become intrigued by how this Baptist society that comprises people on various points of the conservative-progressive spectrum continues to struggle internally with the anti-racism agenda. I have come to understand this as an issue of method (and their implications). In the last two years, I have been developing a programme called Visions of Colour, a resource on anti-racism for Baptist ministers in Britain.[336] I hoped to reflect a multitude of voices in the resource. It was important for the resource to demonstrate a variety of opinions on anti-racism and methods for developing an anti-racist church to reflect the nature of the Baptist landscape best. However, I struggled to get the support/involvement of those who may be considered a more conservative voice (both theologically and politically)[337] in the Baptist Union. While some may believe this is evidence of disinterest, intolerance, or anti-anti-racism, I recognise that the extreme polarisation of opinions, beliefs, and ways of doing theology create a chasm of distrust and frustration. Considering

---

[335] Andy Goodliff, 'What does it mean to be Baptist?', *Baptists Together* (Spring 2021) originally cited in Steven Harmon, *Baptist Identity, and the Ecumenical Future* (Baylor, 2016).

[336] https://www.baptist.org.uk/Groups/379637/Visions_of_Colour.aspx.

[337] Here I assume that theology and politics are very intricately linked, particularly on issues of social justice.

decolonisation as an inevitable development of 'dissenting' can bridge the chasm on an issue both parties (and all in between) consider important to address.

This chapter is not to call out the racists, the 'colour-blind' ultra-conservatives, or the hyper-progressives, but to consider a path toward anti-racism driven by the tradition (and theology) of radical dissent and the method of de-colonisation. This central principle brings together all Baptists along this invisible spectrum of opinion, belief, philosophy, and method that undergird their personal and communal theologies.

Radical Dissenters in this context refer to those seeking to reflect Christ in action, epistemology, and belief, setting themselves apart from society and other religions.[338] Historically, we know that protestant dissenters were Christian believers who pulled away and separated themselves from the European church-state hierarchical Bible religion to rediscover a Christianity that sought to maintain continuity with the early Christian Church and grapple with Christ's teaching on personal salvation, social activism, and the authority of scripture. William Brackney, in *The Spirit Among the Dissenters,* succinctly describes the nature, experience, and legacies of dissenters. He says,

---

[338] Nigel Wright, *Baptist Basics: Radical Dissent* (Baptist Union of Great Britain, 2016). Available at: https://www.baptist.org.uk/Publisher/File.aspx?ID=168469&view=browser [Accessed, June 2021].

Dissenters are interesting people on the canvas of history. They work beyond boundaries, fall below the expectations of the mainstream, or deliberately call into question a prevailing idea or rule. They may deliberately claim the posture of a 'dissenter,' or they may be so classified by someone within the mainstream context. Across the history of the church, some dissenters have suffered extreme exclusion, only to be 'restored' later, such as the second century Montanists.[339]

This definition helps consider the connections between dissenters and decolonisers; it describes those who go against the grain, a minority effort that seeks to preserve and liberate a tradition, a way of life and a divine commission despite its transformations over centuries. Decolonisation is most integrally understood as a secular philosophy rooted in the ongoing emancipation from colonialism in nationalist and epistemological terms (decoloniality). Bridges between this political/philosophical endeavour and Christian theologies have emerged — an effort to decolonise the Christian faith or religion from the usurping epistemic authority of colonial Christianity, which requires re-reading the Bible and resisting European normativity as authoritative in interpretation. I refer to the three P's that surmise key objectives of decolonisation:

---

[339] William H. Brackney, *The Spirit Among the Dissenters: Other voices in understanding the Spirit of God* (Eugene, OR: Cascade, 2019), xiv.

Power — Decolonisation calls for the dismantling or reforming of historic colonial structures and institutions to share power among all participants from all communities.

Presence — Decolonisation calls for the recognition of the presence of the 'other': non-white peoples that have made significant contributions to the shaping of society in the case of British contexts. It also considers ways in which the presence of the 'other' critiques the existing power structures.

Participation — Decolonisation demands a seat at the table for the 'other' to meaningfully shape their experiences in society. This approach would be an equal contribution in a space that accepts contextualised and nuanced presuppositions, knowledge forms and outcomes.[340]

One of the challenges with decoloniality for Christian thinking is the demands that key decolonial theorists have made for true decoloniality — I think of pluriversality,[341] whereby truth is local and contextual. In this paradigm, a universal perspective of truth is considered coloniality.[342] The decolonial space is generally

---

[340] E. P. Louis, *Black, British and De-Churched: a critical investigation of conservative Bible reading groups and Afroasiatic diasporic religious movements in London*. (PhD, Canterbury Christ Church University, 2021).

[341] Bernd Reiter, *Pluriverse: The Geopolitics of Knowledge* (Durham: Duke University Press, 2018).

[342] Anibal Quijano and Michael Ennis Michael, 'Coloniality of Power, Eurocentrism, and Latin America', *Neplantla: Views from the South* 1.3 (2000): 533-80.

understood to house a variety of truths dependent on one's experience of colonialism; this applies to methods of decolonisation — a truth with parenthesis. Mignolo suggests 'truth without parenthesis is war'; truth without the clarifying clause, be it context, experience, or location, disturbs the potential for people to live in a pluriverse.[343] This concept will be a challenge for many Baptists in Britain when translating this into theological and religious terms, those who believe in a single universal truth, a single route to salvation and the sole authority of Christ as revealed in scripture on the Christian faith. One of the many challenges in engaging others in anti-racism is introducing intentionally contextual theologies[344] when they are usually laden with the 'pluriverse' demand. In this chapter, I want to explore a variation of decoloniality: de-colonisation. Some Black Bible-reading religions seek to de-colonise Christianity or mainstream Bible religion by rejecting the colonial rendition and rediscovering the most accurate and authentic Bible religion. In this sense, they aim to detach (visualise removing someone's hand from an object with force) the grip of colonialism from God-talk, hermeneutics, education, ritual, and day-to-day living — to reveal what is under the big white hand. Admittedly, this is an ambitious venture and perhaps utopic in vision.[345] However, the drive and

---

[343] Walter D. Mignolo, 'The politics of Decolonial Investigations (Theory from the Margins)' (2021) [Accessed 2021] Available at: https://www.youtube.com/watch?v=qDEEbVcxmRU&t=1109s

[344] All theology is contextual.

[345] Postcolonial discourse considers concepts such as 'hybridity' that exists as a result of the permanent impacts of colonialism on a post-colonial society and the emerging cultures that are formed within post-colonial communities.

177

method employed by those belonging to Black Bible religions or those I refer to as the Black, British and de-churched, illuminate a great bridge builder for a Baptist community — the Baptist Union in particular — where theological pluralism is a growing reality (and arguably an essence of Baptist-ness). I will begin by introducing the Black, British and De-churched and argue for their prophetic role as dissenters and de-colonisers in twenty-first-century Western society. I will then consider the common ground between Baptists and the de-churched in their emergence, subversion, and intent to *recover*.

Black, British, and De-churched

'Black, British and De-churched' describes people within the Black-British community who have left mainstream churches and sought (or are seeking) an alternative religious space that engages with their ethnic and cultural identity, social and political needs, and spirituality. The de-churched phenomenon is not a new or an original concept[346] — Ethiopianism, the root of religious

---

This challenges the notion that one can truly return or reconstruct a pre-colonial culture if one has been significantly influenced by a colonial culture.

[346] See Caleb Davis, (2018) 'Understanding the De-churched in your city' [Accessed 2022] Available at: https://www.acts29.com/understanding-and-reaching-the-de-churched-in-your-city/ ; Brian Harris (2015) 'Churched, Unchurched or De-churched' [Accessed 2022] Available at: https://brianharrisauthor.com/churched-un-churched-or-de-churched/ ; and Tom Schultz (2013) 'Why I Never say "Don't serve outside our church"' [Accessed 2022] Available at: https://churchleaders.com/outreach-missions/outreach-missions-articles/171094-thom-schultz-serve-church-outside.html

movements such as Rastafari or the (Black) Hebrew Israelites, has been a theologically subversive force since the nineteenth century (the Black, Atlantic and De-Churched). However, my focus here is on the twenty-first-century exodus of Black people from Christian churches, specifically those who have joined alternative Bible-reading religious spaces. Ethiopianism, from its inception, was concerned about discerning the truth about the God of the Bible; it defied the colonial (mis)reading of the text of which the interpretive frame was White supremacy and sought to discover the God revealed through the writings of Afroasiatic peoples – their ancestors.[347] Thus, it became necessary to read the Bible in a way that rejected the lie of racism and white supremacy and instead recover a religious text that originated in the Afroasiatic region as a religious and cultural asset of their ancestors and extended genealogical family — to see God as the God of the Ethiopians and the Hebrews.

The Black, British De-churched cannot explicitly be considered Christian from a Baptist perspective. Although centred around

---

[347] For further reading please see Asafa Jalata, 'Being in and out of Africa The Impact of Duality of Ethiopianism', *Journal of Black Studies* 40.2 (2009): 189-214; Charle Price, 'Cultural Production of a Black Messiah: Ethiopianism and the Rastafari." *Journal of Africana religions,* 2.3 (2014): 418-33; Charles Price, *Becoming Rasta: Origins of Identity in Jamaica* (New York: New York University Press, 2009); James Quirin, 'W.E.B. Du Bois, Ethiopianism and Ethiopia, 1890-1955', *International Journal of Ethiopian Studies* 5.2 (2011): 1-26; George Shepperson, 'Ethiopianism and African Nationalism', *Phylon* (1940-1956), 14.1 (1953): 9-18; Robbie Shilliam, 'Ethiopianism, Englishness, Britishness: struggles over imperial belonging', *Citizenship Studies* 20.2 (2016): 243-59.

biblical teachings and most adherents regarding the Bible in its original form as the highest authority on religious life, many within the community of the de-churched have become estranged from the idea that Yeshua is God-incarnate.

The de-churched seek a space where they do not have to theologically, culturally, and socially conform to the mainstream baseline and interrogate core doctrinal and theological positions that appear to stem from the white mainstream church. This pursuit for liberty has birthed Afroasiatic-diasporic religions such as the Rastafari, The Nation of Islam, the Holy Qubtic Church and (Black) Hebrew-Israelite communities. By re-reading the Bible and resisting the historical colonial christianisation of the ancestors, these communities see the Bible as an Afroasiatic historical religious artefact – the property of their ancestors reappropriated for white domination.

Although the de-churched[348] now experience Christianity in a new twenty-first-century context — living in Britain and as free citizens — the legacy of colonial Christianity, as exposed by key figures such as Leo Muhammad[349], Elder Nathaniel[350] and Kahun

---

[348] My use of the term de-churched is not considering an involuntary, accidental, or passive (choose different word) action of leaving the Church, but an intentional unplugging from the mainstream institution and rejection of its value and authority as far as it is related to God's unfolding redemption plan.

[349] Leader of the Nation of Islam in the UK.

[350] Leader of Israel United in Christ, a (Black) Hebrew Israelite community based in the US but with chapters in Britain.

Montu Tar (Dr Horace Wright),[351] continues to prompt basic three questions:

1. What is the truth about God, Jesus, and the Bible?
2. Where can this truth be located?
3. How can we discern the truth from the lie of colonial Christianity and the growing influence of humanism and anti-religious ideology?

Of course, these questions are not new; all people, from all places and at all times, ask questions along these lines – and all people ask them in context – in their context. The context in which these questions arise for the Black, British and De-churched are of being from minority communities in the nation-state of their historical enslavers, colonisers and Christianisers. These questions, in this context, are asked by those who seek to worship God, adhere to the teachings, instruction and insights of the Biblical texts (to varying degrees), and yet detach themselves from the bible-religion that has been the product of Constantine's Christianisation and the legacies of Roman-centric domination that then became Euro-centric as the colonial powers shifted between the various European nations. Jerome Gay is a witness to this phenomenon in the United States; he says,

> The whitewashing of Christianity and its Eurocentric focus has led to a growing sentiment among people of African descent, as well as people across the globe, that

---

[351] Priest of the Holy Qubtic Church in London.

> Christianity is a Western-created, European-influenced, white-owned religion of oppression . . . The main reason for this growing sentiment is historical and cultural whitewashing, as well as the under-emphasised reality that the Gospel took firm root in Africa, the Middle East, and Asia long before it reached the West.[352]

The mainstream Church then, in this light, symbolises white power, colonialism, and exploitation. Consequentially, liberation for Black and Brown people is to 'de-church' from this white religious-political monster. A common trend among the de-church is to reconnect with Afroasiatic religious roots that do not minimise ethnic and cultural particularities but instead embrace them to reflect what they can see in the Bible. An example of this is demonstrated by the Holy Qubtic Church, which believes and teaches that the original Bible belong to the Ta-ma Reans (Ancient Africans):

> The Intense Scriptural-Study Parchments also allow each who reads them, especially those of the Nubian-Melaninite family, to regain a sense of self-pride, responsibility to the betterment of humanity, along with the knowledge as to the Tama-Rean (Ancient African) perspective of the scriptures of old, and just how those precepts were misinterpreted to the point whereby

---

[352] Jerome Gay, 'All White Everything' in *Black Urban Apologetics: Restoring Black Dignity with the Gospel* edited by Eric Mason (Grand Rapids: Zondervan, 2021) 15.

they became concepts which are now more so Greco-Roman in appearance and teachings, than Tama-Rean (Ancient African). This causes so many, especially those of the Nubian-Melaninite family, to feel a lack of direct-connection to divinity, possessed by a sense of self-hate, or worse, end up totally giving up on the realities of the Scriptures as they feel there is no place for them in the world of spirituality called religion as it is being taught and accepted in this day.[353]

For many of the de-churched I have encountered, Christianity has significantly influenced their family's lives since childhood and is a major part of their identity formation. The process of achieving a de-colonised Bible religion has been to rediscover pre-colonial identities of those now known as Black there is much overlap in approach between Afroasiatic Diasporic Religions[354] and Afrocentrism, Pan-Africanism, and Black consciousness movements.[355] To de-colonise is to sever ties completely with

---

[353] https://journeyhomegroup.com/about [Accessed October 2021]

[354] I use Afroasiatic Diasporic Religions to describe religions that were birthed in the African diaspora postcolonialism but whose mythical and genealogical roots are in the Afroasiatic region such as Rastafari, (Black) Hebrew Israelites, the Nation of Islam and the Holy Qubtic Church. But for this chapter I stick the more conventional term 'black bible religion'

[355] 'Black consciousness refers to the intentional social, cultural, religious, and political effort of a person or people to explore and embody 'Blackness' in all its diversity, evolution, and complexity. This Black consciousness directly responds to an identity crisis within Black diasporic and African peoples resulting from enslavement, colonisation, and Christianisation. It is both connecting with the past (pre-enslavement/colonisation) and carving out the

colonial Christianity and to acknowledge the Bible religion's true origins as a cultural and religious asset of the Afroasiatic region (ethnic, genealogical, and geographic) and, therefore, the authority for understanding the text to be found among the people (and their ancestors) from within those regions.

In *What Colour is your God?: Black Consciousness and the Christian Faith,* the authors demonstrate the dissenting quality that is birthed from the dissatisfaction with mainstream Christianity:

> We've seen that Black Consciousness also lays the basis and creates the desire for new Black religious experience and expression. Those who criticise and fear Black consciousness because of its implications of what religion should be for the new Black person fail to comprehend the potentially positive religious forces which Black consciousness precipitates.[356]

---

future for healthy Black identity/ies across the Black Atlantic, hoping that this process will contribute to the betterment of Black life in all spheres of life. Beyond Afroasiatic Diasporic Religions, Black consciousness may be reflected in Pan-Africanism, Black Nationalism, Afrocentrism, and other more nuanced expressions.' A quote from Louis, (2020) 'Black, British and De-Churched: a critical investigation of conservative Bible reading groups and Afroasiatic diasporic religious movements in London.', [Unpublished Doctoral Thesis submitted to Canterbury Christ Church University] p.16.

[356] Colombus Salley and Ronald Behm, *What Colour is your God?: Black Consciousness and the Christian Faith* (New York: Citadel Press, 1988), 80.

The force of Black consciousness, the awakening force, is usually known as 'woke' (despite its white progressive appropriation and right conservative denigration) — it fuels the De-churched. It causes them to have dissented from the mainstream Church and seek to experience something new by recovering a lost Afroasiatic Bible religion.

Baptists and the Black, British De-Churched: Common Ground

The Black, British and De-church peoples have much in common with protestant and Baptist dissenters. This section will briefly reflect on three ways these two religious groups share common ground: the emergence of the Bible-based movements, how they operate subversively, and finally, the notion of *recovering* the essence of ancient Christianity.

From a religious studies perspective, the Christian traditions that emerged from the Reformation and the formation of dissenters — protestants — can be viewed as New Religious Movements. J. Gordon Melton suggests that NRM are recognised by their relationship to the religion they emerged from the larger and more established religious institution.[357] Seeing the Reformation and the subsequent protestant traditions in this frame illuminates religion's ever-reforming and reframing nature and its relationship to society's political and social climate. Claims that some aspects of Christianity are overly spiritual, separatist and seek to distance themselves from socio-political issues are

---

[357] See J. Gordon Melton, *The Encyclopedia Of Religious Phenomena* (Canton, MI: Visible Ink: 2007).

contested if we consider their method, structure, and mission contextually.

In *A Question of Identity*, Brian Haymes says, 'Baptists are, historically, part of the fruit of that strong tree called the Reformation. We gladly take upon our lips the evangelical doctrines of justification by grace through faith alone. We are protestants and not a little proud of it.'[358] In this work, Haymes presents three historical Baptists that 'express the tradition of dissent.'[359] Thomas Helwys was among the first to have established a Baptist Church on British soil, William Knibb, a missionary, and abolitionist posted in Jamaica, and Martin Luther King Jr, a minister and activist whose efforts were crucial to the civil rights movement in North America. Haymes posits, or perhaps reminds Baptists, through the legacies of these Baptists, that we have social concerns and responsibilities: 'what of our commitment to the prophetic dream, to social righteousness, to a new and just social order?'[360] Haymes challenges Baptists to see dissent not just as a historical event but as an ongoing call to action — to participate and de-participate from evil and pseudo-authorities over the Church and signify one's commitment to Christ the redeemer through ongoing dissent that has social, political, economic, and I would add cultural, ramifications. The context within which historical dissent has been actioned is

---

[358] Brian Haymes, 'A Question of Identity: Reflections on Baptist Principles and Practice', *Journal of Baptist Theology in Context* 4 (2021): 28.

[359] Haymes, 'A Question of Identity', 34.

[360] Haymes, 'A Question of Identity', 35.

important — dissenting is not driven purely by a spiritual image of the true Church but is in response to contextual evils in the every day, the usurping of the authority of Christ, the oppression of underdog communities, economic exploitation and cultural cannibalism that purports the superiority of one group of people over another.

Through their actions of revolt, rebellion and reform, and teaching and interpretation of scripture, Martin Luther King Jr and Sam Sharpe[361] are prime examples of the very *Baptist* dissent-decolonisation bridge. Many have learned the nuances of their theological trajectories through the writing and thinking of many (but not all) Black Baptists in recent history — Black Liberation Theology and Womanist Theologies. Although many Conservative Baptists may reject the philosophical or methodological premise upon which Black Liberation and Womanist theologies rely — recognising the contextual outworking of decolonial-dissent in recent history demands pause for thought for all Baptists about the multidimensionality of dissent brought to light by historically oppressed communities.

Dissenters were believers who sought the Church's position in society to be present and active, non-dominating, voluntary and a witness of Christ's redemption, which in theory should oppose the Christianizing force of the Roman church and the unfolding legacy of many protestant divisions. Christ's radical ministry

---

[361] Sam Sharpe was a Baptist deacon, who organized a slave rebellion in Jamaica in 1832.

subverted religious and political authorities through his teaching and ministry among his people, helping his people to rediscover salvation through faith and by grace. It is this method that the notion of 'being a radical dissenter' centres on, not against the idea of authority in general, for Christ was submitted to the will and authority of the Father but against the oppressive human authorities. However, as can be traced in the histories that followed, protestants, although pulling away from the domination of the state-church powers, had not related that element of emancipation and freedom in their missionary work abroad — many non-conformists, dissenting protestants, including Baptists, were indeed a Christianising force throughout the world.

Decolonisation has struggled to realise firm roots in Baptist churches in Britain, which (I understand) has a significant evangelical stance. Discussions about decolonisation and how it can be pursued have deep roots in liberal or progressive scholarship and is, therefore, in tension with core protestant Christian doctrine such as the authority of scripture. As a result, decolonisation is underestimated in its capacity to work well with traditional methods for doing theology, such as apologetics, systematic theology, and exegesis.[362] However, despite the minority approach that seeks to dismantle the existing structures that undergird traditional theological orthodoxy (often considered patriarchal, LGBTQI+ - phobic and whitewashed), the Black

---

[362] These should not be mistaken for being white/European methods for doing theology as these approaches have been performed by African and Asian church fathers during the early church era.

British and De-churched have demonstrated that if we consider Christianity as a Bible religion from the Afroasiatic region, we can quickly discern the conventions that should be considered a European contextual response, syncretism or intentional whitewashing and protect the core doctrines, beliefs and reverence for scripture as was demonstrated by the Messiah.

When looking at both dissent and decolonisation in the context of the Western church, it seems logical to suggest that they are two sides of the same coin. Both are socially conscious, seeking religious freedom and dismantling the usurping power of a human empire over God's church – specifically in the era extending between Luther and the present day it is the European colonial empire.[363] In reference to infamous German reformer and dissenter Martin Luther, Andrew Bradstock reminds us of the ongoing tensions and challenges of realising religious emancipation that has deep and faithful roots in scripture, which is considered ultimately authoritative and sacred.

Though politically Luther might be deemed conservative and reactionary, his theological discovery has led to his being hailed as an early figure in the development of modern democracy.[364] In his radical boldness, Luther was a part of birthing something new in European society, a new system that, despite his conservative

---

[363] Its many shades, phases, and shifts.

[364] Andrew Bradstock, 'The Reformation' in *The Wiley Blackwell Companion to Political theology* edited by William T. Cavanaugh and Peter Manly Scott. Second Edition. (New Jersey: Wiley, 2018), 68.

stance, challenged and reformed a pre-existing system seeking empowerment and participation for the everyday person. Luther faced much criticism for promoting 'quietism' and passivity in the face of tyranny,[365] despite his crucial role in the Reformation, but there is, of course, Reformation beyond Luther. His deep-rooted deference to tradition and institution may be a form of conservatism that had stifled his ability to see the full potential for emancipation theologically and the need for force (which he would consider rebellion and others may call self-defence[366]); one should not negate the core values of the Reformation and Luther's dissenting victory.

At the centre of the Reformation and the dissent from a dominating and exploitative religion is the recognition of the equality with which all people have access to salvation through grace – not means or ethnicity. This challenge to the church-state is, to the reformers, the recovery of the true faith and Christian principles outlined in the Bible. So, whilst one politicises Luther and his contribution to the Reformation through a (contemporary) radical liberatory lens, it is preserving the religion as reformers believed it had been before Roman colonisation.

This brings us to the question of what it means to be radical — there is not enough space in this chapter to have an extensive discussion, but a quick diversion affords one a moment of pause.

---

[365] Bradstock, 'The Reformation', 70.

[366] Se Devon Dick, *The Cross and the Machete: Natives Baptists of Jamaica*. Kingston: Ian Randle, 2011).

Kehinde Andrews says, 'Radicalism is based on rejecting the fundamental principles that govern society and creating a new paradigm.'[367] This definition echoes the beliefs of many decolonial scholars and activists who are considering how new ways of thinking, relating to one another, knowing (epistemology), and new social structures are where hope for true liberation for all in society lies. However, Nigel Wright on Radical Dissent[368] argues 'radical' is about doing 'Jesus' rather than something completely new; it is non-conforming to the world but embodying the teachings of Jesus, a genuinely counter-cultural ministry to society.[369] Baptist radical dissent follows the trajectory of the Reformation's heart, resisting an involuntary, dogmatic, and ritual religion. As a result, we have two fundamental principles: A free society and free church. Wright says,

> The State is created to serve God and for the good of humankind. It does its best when it does not claim too much for itself, when it sees itself as a servant and when it does not attempt to impose a religious ideology upon

---

[367] Kehinde Andrews, *Back to Black: Retelling Black Radicalism for the 21st Century* (London: Zed Books, 2018), xviii.

[368] Wright, *Baptist Basics: Radical Dissent*.

[369] I would like to acknowledge the need for further conversations about what 'doing Jesus' looks like contextually and if that in fact fits into the definitions of pluriversality. I would argue not so, that Christ's revelation and route to redemption are not defined by contexts but may be expressed and understood with contextual nuance. This chapter cannot afford this significant diversion.

191

people. The State can at times exalt itself into an idol or it can at other times use religion to justify illegitimate power. A radical dissenting position argues that the State best serves God and humankind when it fosters religious liberty and other freedoms, and especially when it respects and protects the rights of minority groups. It should be understood that this approach is based on the confident belief that because the gospel is true and can look after itself, it does not need to be bolstered by State power or given preferential treatment.[370]

The difference between the (documented) Baptist view and popular progressive ideals is the approach to changing that status quo. As per Kehinde and others, Radicalism requires a complete overhaul, whereas the reformed view is to *recover* what has been outlined in scripture and not designed by humanity. Michael Haykin attests to this when considering the theological processes of the Baptist's predecessors,

> Among the Puritans, it was a common assumption that careful study of the New Testament would yield a blueprint by means of which the Church could be reconstituted. Although they differed on the details of this blueprint, they were fundamentally agreed that such a blueprint did exist. One significant consequence of this assumption was that once this blueprint was believed to have been discovered and the Church reconstructed

---

[370] Wright, *Baptist Basics: Radical Dissent*, 5.

accordingly, it could only be considered a betrayal of fellowship if there was any fraternisation with churches that refused to be reformed according to the details of the blueprint.[371]

Afroasiatic Diasporic Religions show a similar attitude toward decolonisation in that they look to scripture to design a nation that belongs to God. An example can be found on the website of an Israelite community called Israel United in Christ, one of the world's most prominent (black) Hebrew Israelite communities. In this section on 'beliefs', they state:

WE ARE THE CHOSEN

As a faith-based organization, our core values and principles are deeply rooted in these divine and sacred scriptural writings specifically from the original 1611 KJV Bible. Again, our entire belief system is not of our agenda but rather God's agenda. We do not pick and choose which scriptures to follow, as does the Christian church. We take heed to every single book in the Bible from Genesis to Revelation, including the Apocryphal ancient books originally published in the original 1611 King James Bible which were later removed.

Consequently, we are returning to the ways of our forefathers in every single aspect of our lives as we learn

---

[371] Michael A. G. Haykin, 'The Baptist Identity: A view from the Eighteenth Century', *Evangelical Quarterly* 67:2 (1995): 138-39.

and teach our people what the Most High requires of us. Through our teachings, each and every day we strive and endeavor to reclaim and restore our identity, our history, our culture, and the traditions of our forefathers which were all stripped away from us as a result of slavery. We are rebuilding our nation; recovering and regathering the diaspora, the remnant of our people scattered throughout the world and teaching them that they are the true Israelites according to the Bible.[372]

Whilst nationalism (and also nationalism as a fruit of colonialism), supremacy and separatism are often concerns for many who, across material such as this, the method to achieving a God-centred society illuminated one of many connections between early radical dissenting Baptists and those among the Black, British and De-churched. Recovering the design as written in scripture during the time of the early reformers and those experiencing racial terror by Catholic and Protestant state powers required undermining these very structures and (re)emerging as a priesthood of (all) believers.

Radical, dissenting Baptists and many within the Black, British and De-churched community who have left mainstream churches and joined Black Bible religions in Britain share a similar historical and theological trend. I seek not to over-extend the commonalities, as there are also many points of divergence and conflict (socially and theologically speaking). However, briefly

---

[372] http://israelunite.org/about-iuic/beliefs/ [Accessed October 2022}

considering the emergence, subversion, and recovery of what is true concerning Christianity as a Bible religion demonstrates how dissent and decolonisation are synergistic.

Conclusion

Twenty-first-century conversations about identity have raised crucial issues for many Christian communities. On the topic of race and racism, much of the social progress is being trailblazed by groups outside of the Church, many of which hold British churches to account for complicity in historic terror and exploitation but also in present-day complicity through its teaching, preaching, aesthetics, colour-blind theology, and silence.

Although not a new topic, Critical Race Theory has become topical among Baptists in Britain, with many embracing CRT as a methodological tool for illuminating the sin of racism. Others remain suspicious of this secular endeavour, particularly its use in the postcolonial and liberationist traditions that criticise and challenge the authority and meanings of the Scriptures. Therefore, it has been a challenge for the British churches to interrogate the legacies of colonialism that affect present-day attitudes and resistance to the changes that must occur when taking the cries of the oppressed seriously.

The understated connection between the dissent and decolonisation – that both reject oppressive church-state powers - considered conceptually and historically; there is much overlap in the agenda – yet as terms, such as radical and decolonial, often belong in the pool of progressive or liberal scholarship there is one agenda that is over-looked. The agenda to correct – the agenda of pluriversality hides the dissenters' and the de-colonisers' natural proclivity to correct wrongs, to challenge lies and uncover hidden truths. The pursuit of anti-racism -the intentional actions that challenge racism, embodies all that dissent and decolonisation offer when considered historically and conceptually.

This chapter posits that decolonisation is a natural outcome of the Baptist principal *Dissent*, and this is supported by considering another dissenting movement - the Black, British and de-churched. This community demonstrates how the principle of dissent, along with the initial ideals that drove the protestants centuries ago, demands a process of decolonisation. This chapter considers how radical dissent and decolonisation are effective mechanisms for religious identity formation, from which racial justice is inevitable. Finally, I suggest that further enquiry into the Black British de-churched can help to remind Baptists of how radical dissent continues to live on and speak prophetically into twenty-first-century British society.

8. Amber-tinted Spectacles: Learning to Live with Lament

Tim Judson

In the short period of time that I have been studying theology, I have come to appreciate the move in many fields of the discipline towards a necessary contextualisation in terms of how we think about God, ourselves, and the world. Some people have always done this. However, many folks (myself included) are coming to recognise the importance of considering one's own disposition and personal narrative when contemplating the being and action of God in the world. Instead of applauding the supposed and prevalent value of objectivity (which is in itself a subjective claim), many pathways, including systematics, are doing important work regarding the embodied reality of human horizons as we attempt to craft human words that point humbly and hopefully towards the self-revealed Word of God. Our ultimate reference point is, of course, God's enfleshed Word, who is the true witness of God, spoken within a particular human form, temporally, spatially, contextually, that is, incarnationally. In other words, being a Christian means delving ever more deeply into the reality of (created) human existence, with all its complexities and contingencies, in a fallible effort to know the One who knows and loves each one of us in our particular bodily life. We cannot do this from the cheap seats of observation or from the uncostly illusion of abstract concepts. Talking about God entails a necessary and dynamic consideration of ourselves in all that particularity and messy nuance that takes hard work and makes life together far richer if we have the patience for it.

I believe that this process of contextualisation is harder for people like me. Historically, White men have assumed a posture of objectivity, a self-sufficient introspection that continues to be imitated within theological institutions and churches. This White ghost that we are encouraged to chase at times unintentionally leads us to overlook the particular points of reference which orient our ways and means of doing theology, our blood, the land we live in, and the stories which shape our imaginations. If we can harness the contribution of recent trajectories towards contextualisation, self-reflection, and interdependence, we might be able to celebrate a richer diversity, of which we each constitute a necessary part. But this requires effort and a disarming resistance against many natural impulses, such as pride, insecurity, fear, through humility, openness, questions, and genuine faith.

It would be easier if I could just construct a one-size-fits-all framework from which to get the measure of God and others in the world. I could simply seek the truth of all things in a pious and otherworldly naivety, and once I've grasped that, I could utilise it to ensure that I live a good life and encourage others to adopt that too alongside me, confident that the Bible clearly says what I think the Bible says. However, my own theological epistemology is wrapped up within the God-given limits of my own horizons, which include how I read the Bible for a start. I am not, and nor will I ever be, able to transcend my limitations and specific creaturely existence, and nor should I. There are ways I am socialised, experiences which cultivate my memory bank, spaces I inhabit that have an effect on my body, unseen wonders and menaces that orient my comportment to this creation, stories which tell me who I am and inculcate my daily habits and orientation in the world. I could go on, but the point I want to highlight is that these particular aspects of our identity really are (or can be) a gift, for they are essential to being human. Why would I want to evade the particular limits of who I am unless I was wanting to be something other than a truly free human being? I am not infinite, but finite. I am not the creator but created. Indeed, it is within the specificity of my finite creatureliness that God wants to commune with me, and me with God, in freedom with other free human beings. This is not a doctrinal compromise; it is a recovery of doctrinal faithfulness, a doctrine of creation, christologically grounded, and from my perspective, it touches on the heart of what it means to be Baptist.[373]

---

[373] We believe 'That our Lord and Saviour Jesus Christ, God manifest in the flesh, is the sole and absolute authority in all matters pertaining to faith and practice, as revealed in the Holy Scriptures, and that each Church has liberty, under the guidance of the Holy Spirit, to interpret and administer His laws.' Steve Holmes probably catches this doctrine best, noting the letters to the churches in Revelation 2–3, which have starkly different messages, and yet each in their geographical and ecclesial particularity witness Christ's voice in continuity with the meta-narrative of God's revelation through Holy Scripture. Each has a different message, but not one that conflicts with others. See Stephen R. Holmes, 'Baptist Identity, Once More,' *Journal of Baptist Theology in Context 3* (2021): 21.

The problem comes when we don't navigate this particularity and transience of our existence. If we universalise the optic through which we read the Scriptures, or understand a life of faith in Christ as a static (or dead!) foundation, we craft a theological or biblical universe that we might feel free to dwell in, which makes sense to us, but which enslaves others, coercing or imposing upon them in their particularity making it hard to breathe the free air of the Spirit's life. I am not remotely playing down the universal and absolute lordship or God in Christ, who has reconciled *all things* to God according to his covenant faithfulness.[374] What I am saying is that we must not deify *ourselves* by absolutising *our* ideas or experiences, which inevitably leads to forging a "God" in our own image, funnelling the aseity of the divine through our conceptual apparatus, and compromising the integrity of how faith in God really plays out in human sensibilities and finitude. Jesus is indeed the truth, or at least, I believe so. However, the truth is not an absolute concept, but the living One who is embodied both temporally and spatially as God's own Word, setting us free by the life-giving power of the Holy Spirt when we embrace the truth of *who* He is, as the 'active and direct' lord of us all.[375] In other words, God did not become human so that we could become like God (*sicut deus*), but so that we could become truly human (through Christ) before God and others in the world.[376] I think that we are going in this direction as a Baptist

---

[374] That's how I read Colossians 1:15–20 at least.

[375] Holmes, 'Baptist Identity,' 20–26.

[376] Dietrich Bonhoeffer, *Ethics, Dietrich Bonhoeffer Works*, vol. 6, ed. Clifford J. Green, trans. Reinhard Krauss, Charles C. West and Douglas W.

movement, which is no doubt why there is such a range of voices here in this book. I might not agree with everything here, but that is only half the journey. Walking with others who are different (and even alienated from us) is the heart of the Gospel, and it is why I am honoured to be involved in this project.

There is more I could say about all of this, but in the limited words available, I want to ground this claim about contextualisation by tentatively mapping some of the contours of my own life, sharing a testimony of sorts or a theological reflection, but one which hopefully witnesses to *Jesus* in my life, not the "God" of my experience or imagination, but the One who has become more real than any of that along the way.

Personal Suffering: A Brief Testimony

For a while, I have lived and worked in different marginal communities, learning "from below" how structural initiatives and community relationships sometimes "play out" locally. It has been eye-opening to be alongside those who are homeless, refugees, victims of abuse, those with mental or educational needs, and also living for a time in parts of the Global South. These experiences have deepened my conviction that an attentiveness to issues of justice is within the heartbeat of being a Christian. It is what prompted my PhD studies on the place and meaning of lament for the Christian community in dialogue with Dietrich Bonhoeffer, as I had been concerned for a long time

---

Stott (Minneapolis: Fortress, 2005), 85, 95.

about the severe lack of lament in many congregations.[377] Real people with real problems were finding themselves within the milieu of a Christian community that rarely gave voice, or space, or silence in the face of suffering, sin and sorrow.

Within certain contexts, I personally witnessed the stark separation within physical liturgical spaces whereby those who were "struggling" found themselves sitting on the margins, whilst the seemingly healthy congregated in the centre, and these folks were also the ones "leading" the church. Economic resource, social influence, mental and emotional stability, racial and cultural privilege, these were the veneered mechanisms that carved the shape of the body politic, and this caused me great distress. Some of the means and ways that people sought to "comfort" others who suffered were pastorally questionable and theologically suspect. On one particular occasion, I watched a person who was struggling with depression and suicidal thoughts, being prayed for in a particularly flamboyant way by some of the "leaders," declaring the victory of the cross over their life, triumphantly binding and loosing all sorts of weird and wonderful things in the name of Jesus, and "speaking healing" over this individual. The following week, I was informed that this individual had taken their own life, and we were encouraged to celebrate that they were no longer suffering.

---

[377] See Tim Judson, *Awake in Gethsemane: Bonhoeffer and the Witness of Christian Lament* (Waco, TX: Baylor University Press, 2023).

A few years later, I began ministering in a different church, hoping to never experience something like that ever again. About a month into my new role, I contracted a rare disease called 'Acute posterior multifocal placoid pigment epitheliopathy' (AMPPE). This is an immune-mediated condition that involves inflammation at the back of the eyes, which disrupts the nerves that necessarily enable a person to see. There were huge globs (to use the best word!) in front of my eyes, huge patches of absolute nothingness where I would normally trace colour, shape, depth, and other distinctive facets. It is still unresolved as to what "caused" this. My consultant informed me that it is not a direct result of stress but that stress can undoubtedly engender the sort of vulnerability to things like this, and I had, for various reasons, been extremely stressed.

Whilst my experience was really difficult, I have to confess that it was made harder to bear it due to the "comfort" that was being offered by people in my congregation. It is only by looking back now that I am able to appreciate more fully how well-intentioned my sisters and brothers were. However, at the time, it was anything but helpful. In fact, more often than not, silently bearing people's attempts to support me felt more like an exercise of trying to encourage people that they were encouraging me. It was exhausting, and it was kaleidoscopically frustrating, given the breadth of theological perspectives.

On one occasion, some folks adamantly formed a "prophetic circle" around me, told me to confess my sins, and then proceeded to cast out any demons or unclean spirits that might be "on" me.

They also blessed me with wholeness and healing, demanding in the name of Jesus that I was healed, in a prophet-of-Baal-like enthusiasm. When I opened my eyes, I was almost convinced that I was healed due to their confidence, even though nothing had changed. After I shared the disappointing news, they looked at me quizzically, wondering whether I really had repented or whether a particular language or spiritual technique was required. I walked away before they could commence round two.

Another time, I had a warm and kind individual approach me after the Sunday service over coffee. They asked, "How are your eyes?" For the hundredth time that morning, I answered, "Much the same, but thank you for asking." Their response was wise and knowing, according to them at least. "Perhaps God has made this happen to you in order to teach you some humility. I am sure that this testing of your faith will prove fruitful, so you need to rejoice in this and thank God that in his sovereign will he has caused such a thing." I get what they meant; I really do, and I appreciate what they were attempting for my sake. However, I felt like vomiting.

Maybe this whole illness was God genuinely doing something in a way that I could not yet *see* (pun intended). Alternatively, perhaps this was an assault on my being from forces that were not commensurate with God's intention for my life. Sometimes, illness comes not because of God, nor because of random contingency, but because the world around us assails our limitations and affects us in ways that are damaging. I am still not sure what led to this, but could not rule such a possibility out. For me, it was not remotely clear as to *why* this was happening, and I certainly did not want to limit God (or myself) to a posture of celebration over my temporary loss of sight.

One Sunday, I was preaching on Matthew 4:23–25, and remarked on the difficulty I had with the verse, 'Jesus went throughout Galilee, teaching in their synagogues and proclaiming the good news of the kingdom and curing *every* disease and *every* sickness among the people.'[378] I remarked that I believe Jesus can heal (and I meant this in both an individually miraculous and in a broader, socio-political and salvific sense), but that I found it difficult because I had not fully recovered my sight. As a response, someone shared a testimony of healing that they had experienced. I was sat with a woman who had been hunched over for years, bearing excruciating pain and feeling shunned in the community as a result. The person at the front witnessed to us that God had healed them (and Hallelujah to that!) and went on to ensure me, in all sincerity, that God would therefore heal my eyes as well. Both myself and the woman beside me tried to breathe deeply, but it is hard to do that when you are forcing a smile.

A last scenario involved a group of people at the pub who really felt for me and were deeply concerned, though they dared not try and relate to my predicament. In fact, they thought it was awful, absolutely devastating, which led them to question why God

---

[378] One thing I mentioned was the particular interpretations of πᾶσαν ("every" or "every kind of"). In my view, a helpful perspective on this is offered by Brian Brock, *Wondrously Wounded: theology, disability, and the body of Christ* (Waco, TX: Baylor University Press, 2019), 20.

would ever let something like this happen. "Tim, this is so shit! It must really rock your faith. It's really rocking mine. I don't know if I can even believe in God anymore." Rather than trivialising my pain, these people struggled to reconcile my situation with their (and my) belief in God, as though faith *in God* somehow ultimately depends on our ability to believe. I never doubted God in this. What I needed to do was to ask God *who* God is in the midst of this, wrestling with a dynamic experience that I had never navigated before, so I needed space to seek God here and now.

Like many in our great Judeo-Christian tradition, I was given words through the Psalms to pray. Sometimes, this discipline would lead me in words that I would not personally express, but this would prompt me to pray for others or to reflect on the motives and movements of my own heart. Other times, words would lead me in a way that articulated my experience far more deeply and bravely than I would have dared utter in the polite company of others in Christian worship. I feel ashamed and sad that I felt unable, but I am grateful for the strange companionship of the Psalmist during this time. Certain phrases and motifs stuck out in a new way, words which I had read and prayed as was my habit, but which were illuminated in a new way:

I am weary with my moaning; every night I flood my bed with tears; I drench my couch with my weeping. My eyes waste away because of grief; they grow weak because of all my foes.[379]

---

[379] Ps 6:7.

'I am shut in so that I cannot escape;
        my eye grows dim through sorrow.'[380]

'For now we see in a mirror, dimly, but then we will see face to face.'[381]

'For we walk by faith, not by sight.'[382]

'Then Jesus said to him, "What do you want me to do for you?" The blind man said to him, "My teacher, *let me see again*."'[383]

I longed to see again, trusted that the prognosis was pretty good, even though the disease was not well-known. Months passed, and many doses of steroids went through my system in an attempt to calm my body, lest the inflammation in my eyes left any permanent scarring. I wanted to see clearly. I could not see my son's expressions. We had another baby coming, and I wanted to see them. I was hoping, even expecting, that everything would be fine. My eyes have indeed recovered a lot, and I am so grateful. However, I am one of the very rare cases within this already very rare disease where total healing has not happened. I have permanent scarring on my eyes, and whilst I can do a number of things again, I live with the scars, the blurriness, the grey, and the

---

[380] Ps 88:8–9.
[381] 1 Cor 13:12.
[382] 2 Cor 5:7.
[383] Mark 10:51, emphasis mine.

questions surrounding this life-changing event, with its impact on how I operate.

I want to note that my particular experience became a prism through which I noticed things in the Scriptures that I had not given as much attention to as before. These verses and motifs deepened my reflection on my sight, but also, my difficulty to see—as well as my desperate longing to see clearly again—brought a new, tangible context to how I read these parts of Scripture. It is not that my previous reading was wrong necessarily, but my particular life and context now grappled in a dynamic way with the Scriptures. The Holy Spirit breathed through them as I listened (because I could not read), grounding me in God's Word anew. I often wear amber-lensed glasses now, which take the edge off light contrasts and somehow enable me to read a bit more easily. I guess I now see life through amber-tinted spectacles, whatever that means!

Something that helped me during this period was something from the fourth volume of Karl Barth's *Church Dogmatics*. This might not seem an obvious place to find help in the midst of so traumatic an experience, but much to my surprise, it was. Plus, as the unfinished fragment, *CD* IV/4 would testify, as given the premise behind this book, Barth is really a Baptist![384] I remembered reading a section within *CD* IV/3.2, where Barth offers a four-part

---

[384] Karl Barth, *Church Dogmatics CD* IV/4, trans. Geoffrey Bromiley (Edinburgh: T&T Clark, 2004), 41–213. (Henceforth *CD*).

excursus on the book of Job.[385] I do not find Barth easy to read (and literally could not for many months during this time), but in reflecting and then preaching on this excursus, I came to contemplate the possibility that God is far more real than I (and others) dare to believe. The "God" we tend to talk about in relation to suffering can often cause more harm than good despite our genuinely heartfelt attempts to be faithful. The real (that is, the biblical) God is not the sum of our *ideas* or *experiences*. God is more real than our summations and explanations. Barth helped me to realise that God is far more real than that.

Barth claims that, in subtle yet unmistakable ways, Job resembles Jesus Christ, who is the true witness to God, in contrast to others who can only witness to the one who is his own self-witness. The first two chapters of Job are hugely intriguing, but the events that occur include illness, physical suffering, natural disasters, murder, and huge range of awful events. Following this horrendous sequence of events which befall him, Job laments as a fallible, yet free servant of the free, infallible God.[386] What has been a breakthrough for me in terms of my own formation has been to reflect on the sociality of this book and the strange conflict that arises between Job and his "friends" in the midst of his pain.

---

[385] Karl Barth, *CD* IV/3.2, 383–88, 398–408, 421–34, 453–61.
[386] Barth, *CD* IV/3.2, 384–85.

For Barth, there is nothing wrong with what Job's friends say, at least if we consider their statements propositionally. Their arguments are "sound," and yet Job 'sovereignly ignores' them and persists in his complaint until he hears from God. What is fascinating, and kind of bizarre for many of us, is that God's wrath is eventually kindled not towards Job but with his friends.[387] God arrives to challenge Job, to spar with him, to confront him, to which Job responds in penitence and humility. But God is livid with these so-called "comforters" because they 'have not spoken of me what is right, as my servant Job has.'[388]

Now let's just rewind for a moment. What on earth did they say which was so wrong? I'm pretty sure they were orthodox in their claims, offering sound teaching to the poor, wayward Job as he risked veering off course in his faith. Barth helpfully summarises that they are right in their theological propositions, most emphatically, in their claim that 'whether or not man understands and approves it concretely, God in His sovereign over-ruling is always holy, righteous and wise, and therefore is always to be glorified.'[389] Barth also highlights their appeal to God's rewarding of all people according to their works, that is, mercy for the pious and destruction for the godless, that no one is ultimately righteous before God, that no one should rebel or

---

[387] Barth, *CD* IV/3.2, 455.
[388] Job 42:7.
[389] Barth, *CD* IV/3.2, 454.

complain against His judgments, that one should cling to Him all the more when disaster strikes. After all, 'the God who makes sore also binds up, that the God who wounds also heals, that from Him there may definitely be expected final deliverance from every need, redemption from death and a happy issue to all affliction.'[390] Evil and suffering are only temporal; human wisdom is nothing in light of God's eternal knowledge; our notions of justice are relative in light of the divine creator, which should only humble all who wish to be faithful.[391] Well, what can you say to that? It seems a pretty reasonable reflection of the Old and New Testament message. In fact, 'when *Yahweh* speaks His concluding Word, is not Job actually brought very close to the point which Eliphaz, Bildad and Zophar obviously have in view and to which they try very earnestly if unsuccessfully to direct him?'[392] It would seem that the friends are right, and Job is wrong, as though it all makes perfect sense for them that Job has lost his way. But no. At the end, God reveals a different verdict.

For Barth, this is because Job's friends perceive God as an open book who is bound to the confines of their imaginative possibilities based on previous information they have gained through experience or tradition. Job becomes increasingly obstinate, maybe even heretical, and they are compelled to clarify (on God's behalf of course) who God *really* is.[393] They regurgitate

---

[390] Barth, *CD* IV/3.2, 454.
[391] Barth, *CD* IV/3.2, 455.
[392] Barth, *CD* IV/3.2, 455.
[393] Barth, *CD* IV/3.2, 456–57.

'timeless truths' and systematise God's otherwise free relation to humanity. God is co-opted into a comprehensible religious framework about "God" which Job clearly threatens with his free complaint. He risks blowing up their universal rubric, which they have constructed with sincerity and vigour in order to feel assured in their "faith." Job resists their abstractions, so 'they torture him in the very worst fashion that one man can torture another, addressing him as from God, for the sake of God and in the name of God,' and 'burning him at the stake' to 'the greater glory of God.'[394] Their theory of God is just that, a theory. It is static, conceptual (really boring!) and they are utterly false in the way they react to Job. In contrast, Job believes God (and therefore himself) to be in a dynamically free, covenantal relationship. The "comforters" evade the living God for a deity-in-principle (a "God" of religion) who is devoid of any truly free encounter, whereas Job clings to a God who exists in history and is true as he encounters Job in the time and space of that history.[395]

This is why Job's friends might be considered to be right—in the abstract factuality of what they claim and hurl at Job to his detriment—but why they are profoundly wrong is because they cannot face the truth of a genuinely free (non-abstract) God and a genuinely free humanity. They offer pithy comebacks of a religious "God" (at their disposal) constructed by their 'brittle ideological web of falsehood.'[396] They thereby attack Job's

---

[394] Barth, *CD* IV/3.2, 457.

[395] Barth, *CD* IV/3.2, 458.

[396] Susannah Ticciati, *Job and the Disruption of Identity: Reading Beyond*

freedom, which means everything to him, hence his complaint.[397] Barth laments the destructive posture of speaking in conceptual categories, shattering other human beings in the world with the wrongs that are 'so impressively clothed in the garb of that which is right.'[398] Human falsehood is so deceitful that in our attempts to say and do the right thing, to comfort others in their suffering, we may offer a counterfeit God against their laments, rather than believing in a free relationship with the living God that lives, breathes, bleeds and screams in the darkest shadows of worldly existence. Universally valid platitudes are a toxic medicine for those who suffer like Job, whilst rhetoric like his will only offend and land awkwardly with those who insist on defending "God's" wisdom on "God's" behalf.

Have you ever met someone who is really overwhelmed, depressed, and even at the point of giving up? I'm sure you have, as have I. I confess that I have sometimes found myself unable to even feel anything due to the heavy weight of despair I have been carrying. From what I have experienced, read, or heard, hearing classic biblical "encouragements" does not actually encourage many of us who, for different reasons, are locked inside ourselves. We are not struggling to believe these things conceptually, but concepts do not help in the context of utter despondence. The idea of water does not satisfy a thirsty person but insults the reality that is their existential drought. When the "rich tapestry of life"

Barth (London: T&T Clark, 2005), 163.

[397] Barth *CD* IV/3.2, 460–61.

[398] Barth, *CD* IV/3.2, 459.

disrupts our faith by rupturing the ground beneath our feet, we do not seek a God who is present in the form of pithy sayings and others' own experiences of consolation. We long for, and dare to wait for, the God who is present in this apparent absence.[399] We require time and space to retain assurance of our humanity in these experiences of godforsakenness, and sometimes, this can only be ensured through the unconventionality of lament. It takes a lot of vulnerability and courage as we risk being strangled to death by the pious imposition of others' platitudes. It also requires a lot of humility on the part of those who would seek to offer genuine comfort to those who suffer.[400]

Linked to this falsehood is the sloth with which Job's friends maintain a stature of distance and self-preservation. They do not speak solely on an intellectual level but emotionally and morally as well. They genuinely feel for Job, but they are perhaps "worried about him" because he is "in a bad place" and "needs to know God's joy." However, they are basically being lazy and indolent, shirking their responsibility as neighbours, which helps them remain 'unaffected by the despairing struggle for the knowledge of God into which Job finds himself plunged by what has befallen

---

[399] Even as I write this, I am conscious that what I and (what I suggest) others need could be too easily synthesised into a framework for how to "comfort" people. The key thing is not confining people who suffer, and thereby not confining the God who is revealed in suffering.

[400] For a brilliant, personal reflection on this, see John E. Colwell, *Why Have You Forsaken Me?: A Personal Reflection on the Experience of Desolation* (Milton Keynes: Paternoster, 2009).

him.'[401] They retreat inside an introspective cocoon by disregarding his and their humanity. Instead of formation, they offer information. Instead of free humanity, they offer an abstract ethic which always falls short of embodiment. Instead of being 'pilgrims and companions,'[402] they violate Job like marauding, ignorant crusaders. Job is not a distant statistic but a concrete being in their midst, and yet they respond to him with the evil inaction of sloth. They will not continue to mourn with him as he is but are more anxious to defend God, which exposes their fearful inhumanity.[403] Our desire to fix others' problems, like a lot of philanthropy, can end up stifling people's laments, doing more damage and potentially making them either indignant or hopeless. Compassion for others is sometimes rooted in our desire to edify ourselves away from the ambiguity of pain. This is the danger of refusing to be humane alongside others who suffer like Job, and why a preclusion of lament in Christian worship may be more about anxious self-care than faithfulness to Christ.

A haunting example of this would be the historic racism that has stained our country's story. Throughout history, there are examples of the pious, Western church evoking abstract notions

---

[401] Barth, *CD* IV/3.2, 458.

[402] In the Order for Baptist Ministry, of which I am a part, we pray: 'Living God, enable us this day to be pilgrims and companions: committed to the way of Christ, faithful to the call of Christ, discerning the mind of Christ, offering the welcome of Christ, growing in the likeness of Christ, engaging in the mission of Christ, in the world that belongs to Christ.' See 'The Dream,' accessed 16 June 2022, https://www.orderforbaptistministry.co.uk/.

[403] Barth, *CD* IV/3.2, 455. See Rom 12:15–16.

of "providence" in order to make sense of, and therefore somehow justify, the stealing and selling of Black bodies from shore to shore. A doctrine of faith became a doctrine of explanation, and what may have prompted outrage amongst Christ's body, ended up muting it all for the glory of "God."[404] Perhaps imperial Christianity would have benefitted from a stronger *theologia crucis*. Are we discerning our way as Baptists with faithful horizons now that we are no longer "suffering" for our convictions?

As mentioned already, God's wrath is eventually kindled against Job's friends. They can only be saved by giving burnt offerings, and in particular, through Job's intercession on their behalf.[405] Job, the true witness to the true God, is a friend to them in his own service and intercession, even though they have been so sinful in relation towards him. Through their repentance and Job's act, 'They too ... are enfolded by God's active readiness for the remission of sins.'[406] There are salvific implications here. It appears that Job's friends will only receive forgiveness if they confess their sins to Job and ask *him* to pray to God for *them*. Their standing with God is intrinsically bound up in their standing with Job, and this highlights two things. Firstly, as has already been

---

[404] For example, see Willie James Jennings, *The Christian Imagination: Theology and the Origins of Race* (New Haven: Yale University Press, 2010), 16–21. The generational violence this has caused Black bodies is shameful. See Anthony Reddie, *Theologising Brexit: A Liberationist and Postcolonial Critique* (London: Routledge, 2019), 44–51.

[405] Job 42:7–9.

[406] Barth, *CD* IV/3.2, 454.

discussed, we stand under judgment when we silence or rebuke those who cry to God. Secondly, if we do not confess our oftentimes negligent disregard for another's suffering *to them before God*, we may deceive ourselves into thinking the problem is resolved, simply by giving them a tokenistic hearing or confessing to ourselves personally (because that's more British). Sin can convince us that we are reconciled "in theory," whereas Christ actually calls us to be reconciled to him and others in relation to one another through a real, free encounter here and now. Job effectively stands between God and his friends, just as Christ stands between God and us. We see in this passage that those who cause suffering, sometimes in the name of God, need reconciling to God through those they have harmed, however unintentional that was.

The question remains as to the nature of Job's lament itself, which has been disregarded and evaded by his friends. What can people like me learn from Job when we are the individuals or groups who experience suffering personally? For Barth, the basis of Job's complaint is not the loss he has suffered *per se* but the dissonance he faces between his now unbearable existence and his concrete knowledge of God.[407] He encounters God in a way which is utterly alien to what he has previously known, driving him mad with desperation.[408] He cannot withdraw objectively from his situation because he 'can only exist in his suffering,' and as a

---

[407] Kathleen D. Billman and Daniel L. Migliore, *Rachel's Cry: Prayer of Lament and Rebirth of Hope* (Eugene, OR: Wipf and Stock, 1999), 62.

[408] Barth, *CD* IV/3.2, 401–2.

result, he protests against his current existence in relation to God.[409]

Job insistently appeals to God *alone* even though God appears to him (or at least, his experience suggests that God is) a 'relentlessly aggressive adversary ... his most dangerous and implacable enemy.'[410] Job cannot curse God because not even death will separate them. He knows this. It is in dynamic, covenantal proximity to God that Job makes his complaint against God precisely because he does not recognise God here and now in this situation. God does not appear to be the God he concretely knows and believes in. This is why the "God" of his friends is an alien deity because here and now, the real God does not appear in theory but explodes any theological systematisation in world history through a real and terrible encounter which conflicts with his existing (fallible and finite) knowledge. To not cry out in lament over this would be to not believe in the God who faces him now in this incomprehensible and deliberating form. This is an act of true faith and obedience because Job looks to God even though God appears to be and feels like an enemy. Job insists on this God in spite of God's unrecognisability. Job freely wrestles in a violent, conflicting offensive which remains faithful to this God, maintaining his place as God's true witness.[411] He did not give up on God as his wife maybe did (and who would blame her?). Nor

---

[409] Barth, *CD* IV/3.2, 399.

[410] Barth, *CD* IV/3.2, 404.

[411] Barth, *CD* IV/3.2, 405–6. One cannot help but notice the parallels with Jesus in the Garden of Gethsemane.

did he compromise by creating a synthesis of "God" to understand the problem of suffering more easily.[412] To use Barth's words, 'He would not have been obedient if he had not raised this complaint and carried it through to the bitter end in spite of all the objections.'[413]

This is why God concludes that only Job has spoken rightly of him, and why Barth claims we should not go through Job's speech as umpires judging which comments are either laudable or erroneous.[414] Such a task misses the point. Job is put in the right by God because he appeals only and persistently to God and does not seek another "God" or look behind God to exonerate God from any responsibility for his suffering.[415] He demonstrates his freedom for God 'in the violent impatience by which he most seriously jeopardises it.'[416] However, Job is also put in the wrong by God because he advances the claim that God should be his righteous God in a way that Job can register in his fallible finitude. He clings righteously to God alone, but he also wants God to be his God in a manner which is different to that in which God reveals himself to be here and now.[417] 'He rightly maintains his

---

[412] John H. Walton and Tremper Longman III, *How to Read Job* (Downers Grove: Inter Varsity Press, 2015), 95. Also J. Todd Billings, *Rejoicing in Lament* (Grand Rapids, MI: Brazos, 2015), 21; John Swinton, *Raging With Compassion* (London: SCM, 2018), 30–45.

[413] Barth, *CD* IV/3.2, 406.

[414] Barth, *CD* IV/3.2, 406–7. Job 42:7.

[415] Barth, *CD* IV/3.2, 425, also 427.

[416] Barth, *CD* IV/3.2, 407, also 457.

[417] Barth, *CD* IV/3.2, 407.

righteousness before God. But he blatantly sets himself in the wrong by arrogantly advancing that righteousness as a claim that God should be righteous before him, to his human eyes and according to his human thoughts and standards.'[418]

Later, God 'puts him in the wrong but in so doing acknowledges him to be faithful to and in accord with his election.'[419] God does not confirm Job's expectations of who God should be as 'the "God of love and faithfulness" or something similar,' but speaks from within this concealed unknowability, proving that Job was right to appeal to God as this God.[420] Job surrenders any pride he had before God in this regard. His righteous plea—which was a plea finding its basis in God alone—had become his own self-righteousness, for he had judged for himself who God should be. However, as he repents in dust and ashes, he is enfolded within God's freedom towards him, recognising himself to be in the wrong, which is the very admission with which 'God recognises him as His servant who has remained faithful to Him and proved his faithfulness afresh by this very admission.'[421] One cannot help but wonder whether Job's lament would have been saved from any pride if he had not felt backed against a corner by his well-meaning but false friends.

---

[418] Barth, *CD* IV/3.2, 406.
[419] Barth, *CD* IV/3.2, 423.
[420] Barth, *CD* IV/3.2, 427.
[421] Barth, *CD* IV/3.2, 433.

Barth's excursus on Job offers a phenomenal challenge in terms of how we understand lament as a free act and, indeed, how we live as those in covenant relationship with the living God. In our fallibility, we endanger our freedom if we try to resolve the problem of sin and suffering within ourselves, even in our own knowledge of God. As Christians, we are constantly in danger of veering toward abstraction or generating a universal synthesis which resolves the problem of evil and imprisons God, us, and the world. But God is real, far more real than our own experiences, our thoughts, or any way in which we might somehow try to comprehend the One who cannot be fully comprehended. However feeble or irreverent our laments may be as we wrestle with suffering, such is the pathology of the human condition that sin abounds all the more within any other option. Thus, Barth seems to suggest that lament is the right way to be wrong before God in the midst of sin, suffering and sorrow.

I look back at the situation I had with my eyes. I know that no one intended to cause me harm in their words and actions. Some of these folks are amongst the most decent and caring folks I have met. Yet I do wonder sometimes whether that acute experience may have been less painful if there was a more habituated inclination to not fix, explain, or veer towards introspective doubt. Certain friends were particularly helpful during this time, most notably those for whom suffering was a common feature of life. Those who lived with physical disabilities, marginalisation due to the colour of their skin, inner chaos and mental health issues, and tumultuous personal circumstances, I learnt a lot from those who considered suffering to be something more normative than unusual. These folks had a *habitus* almost instinctively flowing in their bodies that regarded suffering as something that is *borne* faithfully rather than something that is to be *resolved* or *evaded*.[422]

Conclusion: What does this have to do with Being Baptist?

Why do some of us think that our experience somehow is going to be the experience of others? Why do we think we can deduce the mind of the creator?[423] Why do we turn inwards, away from God and others, when suffering occurs, whether it is ours or someone else's? Why do we think that a resurrection life in Christ somehow bypasses worldly suffering? I do not know; I do not see that in the Scriptures, but I am grateful for those who sit on the margins, whose presence and narrative continually disrupt the universal norms which can so easily pervade our theology, ethics, and liturgy.

Anyone who has read to the end of this chapter may be wondering why I'm writing about this in a book on Baptist identity. Well, on one level, I had originally planned on putting something about this in my PhD thesis but then changed the direction of the project. On another level, though, I think Barth captures something of the profound reality of being a Christian. More specifically, he touches on the revelation of God within the particularity of human

---

[422] On *habitus* within Christian formation, see James K. A. Smith, *Imagining the Kingdom: How Worship Works*, (Grand Rapids, MI: Baker Academic, 2013), 82.

[423] Rom 11:34.

life in the world. We cannot simply glean a notion of who God is from experiences, authentic as those experiences may be. God is not confined by our experiences as fallible creatures whose existence is transient and perceived through a lens dimly.

As Baptists, one of our *charisms* is the peculiar gift of the local church, the prophetic presence of the community of believers in a particular time and space. Baptists hold the view that the incarnate, crucified, and resurrected Lord Jesus is enfleshed in local communities, and his mind is discerned within that specific body of people. What Jesus calls us to on one day might change in a year, not in a way that *contradicts* the word of God, but which *dynamically guides us* through multiple contingencies along the way. This may feel precarious for those of us who like a plan and a program. However, if covid-19 has taught the world anything, it is that this world is far more real than our plans can ever accommodate or control because human life was always intended to be constituted in relationship with the real God, who is present in space and time by his life-giving Spirit. Our creaturely finitude requires us to honour God with our particularity, and that means embracing our horizons whilst being attentive to the God who is beyond them.[424] Being a Baptist means that I take others' experiences seriously because, through them, I may witness a God who is more true than my individual mind and heart can grasp.

For example, when meeting a person who is homeless, I would do well not to project narrative assumptions upon them based on

---

[424] See Jennings, *The Christian Imagination*, 259–88.

223

previous experiences, all of which are through a lens. Not all homeless people want money, drugs, or alcohol. Not all homeless people are useless. In fact, there's a guy in our church who, it turns out, is an absolute workhorse and painted half of our building with me after Covid. Someone's present suffering is not necessarily for reasons that we might quickly diagnose. Local Baptist churches like ours have an opportunity to learn the art of being human alongside those who disrupt our assumptions regarding sorrow, suffering, and sin.

On another level, I think continued discussions are necessary in relation to race and racism. I confess that I sometimes struggle to see the problem that my Black sisters and brothers highlight. But my lens continues to inform what I see, and I do not see things clearly. Just because I might have a certain perspective from my own vantage point regarding racism, that does not mean I am right. I'm not being categorically post-modern here; I'm trying to appeal to the particularity of those who are different from me and through whom I have an opportunity to reflect on my limited perspective. If a sister or brother with a different colour of skin struggles where I do not, it isn't necessarily that they are the problem. Perhaps instead, Christ is calling to me through their suffering, offering a humanity that transforms my own to be less absolute and more self-aware, even if I may be unable to reckon fully with that person's theological narrative.

What I am saying here gives a doctrinal precedent for recognising the necessary contextualisation of Scriptural faithfulness for each congregation in our union together as Baptists. This could be taken to justify a sort of being-bound-together in a spirit of "unity" that consists of diametrically opposed views about "crucial" matters.[425] Any sense of unity as an agreed "common ground" would surely render such an appeal to unity as false, given that we would only be united in our mutual isolation.[426] Yet even there, in total alienation from one another, I think reconciliation and unity are possible through the living God. This is the crux of the matter, bearing in mind what Barth interprets from Job. The guy who was perceived to be wrong, unorthodox, fallen, dodgy even, was the one that God vindicated, whilst all the others were condemned, despite their exemplary "faithfulness" to the tradition, the Scriptures, and the theological framework. I don't want to be counted amongst Job's friends when I stand face to face with Jesus Christ, so I will journey with what I know, holding it closely, but loosely, in the certain belief that I dare not be certain in myself that I have grasped this God fully.

---

[425] Of course, what issues we designate as "crucial" are also difficult to agree on. Does being "evangelical" (in its increasingly blurry sense) come before being Baptist, or after? Some would even argue that they can be Baptist and not evangelical. I eagerly await Jeff Jacobson's research on such discussions.

[426] Here, I allude to a different basis for unity, or solidarity, which is prophetically articulated by Bonhoeffer. See Dietrich Bonhoeffer, *Sanctorum Communio: A Theological Study of the Sociology of the Church*, Dietrich Bonhoeffer Works, vol. 1, ed. Clifford J. Green, trans. Reinhard Kraus and Nancy Lukens (Minneapolis: Fortress, 1998), 145–52.

9 Baptist Identity? A Response

Anthony Reddie

Although I was brought up within British Methodism and remain a member of the Methodist church, as a recognised Lay or 'Local' preacher, my family antecedents lie in the Baptist tradition. Both my parents, members of the Windrush Generation, were Baptists when they lived in Jamaica. My parents went back to the Baptist tradition when they returned to Jamaica in 1991 on their retirement. My mother, in particular, was a faithful member of Belle Castle Baptist Church, where she became a Deacon and a regular preacher in what became her pride and joy in later life.

As someone who has Baptistic roots and has many friends within the Baptist tradition, I have long been aware of a series of ongoing dialectics that have struck me as being inimical to Baptist identity in Britain for many years. Speaking as a close friend of the Baptist tradition in the UK, I have been struck by the tensions between the theology and practice of 'being church' in which subsidiarity, egalitarianism, radical equity, and non-hierarchy are essential characteristics of what it means to be Baptistic. One of the reasons why my mother returned to the Baptist tradition upon her return to Jamaica lay in the fact that her local church had the authority to recognise her clear and obvious call to ministry that did not require hierarchical approval, often in the shape of people possessed of class and economic privilege who would often have looked down on a dark-skinned, working-class, Black woman possessed of no formal qualifications.

It has been this form of radical egalitarianism and collectivism that has seen the Baptist tradition become the repository for the development of Black liberation theology in the United States and in Jamaica. In the latter, the country of my parent's birth, the Baptist tradition has the proud reputation of being the 'national church' that underpinned the thrust for Black liberation; it is worth noting that three of the six national heroes in Jamaica are Baptists.

And yet the historical and theological emphases that speak to a church often of the proletariat (in ways that have been more demonstrably true than, say, Methodism) is one that has invariably undercut its own radical roots at the altar of ambiguous local practice. In using the latter term, what I mean to speak to is the prevailing sense that the sanctity of the local church and its independence of thought and action (I am often told that the correct usage is 'interdependence', but I have seen too many 'rogue' local expressions to be convinced that this is not always the case) can militate against its best or better intentions.

Take the issue of gender. British Baptists accepted women preachers and ministers long before Methodists did and certainly well in advance of the Church of England. And yet, in the year in which I worked as a Baptist tutor in Bristol, I witnessed the majority of women struggling to find churches that would admit them as the 'Minister in charge'; many of them either became associate ministers in bigger churches or others finding a route into paid ministry via chaplaincy. The gains of the wider tradition and its egalitarian and inclusive tendencies is undercut by the practice of many churches at the grassroots.

In terms of issues of inclusivity as they relate to ethnicity and cultural backgrounds, once again, one can see this ongoing dialectic. Congregationalism has enabled many Black radicals across the world to find creative space in local churches that contain no explicit hierarchy and to which they are not subject to external forms of authority, and yet British Baptists have produced very little in the way of leadership in terms of Black theology in Britain. A tradition that has asserted its commitment to 'freedom of religion' (as we speak, Regent's Park College, where I work, is hosting a major research project exploring the realities of freedom of religion in the UK) on the basis of its own experiential and existential realities of being persecuted dissenters, often seen as an enemy of the establishment, has also proved to be remarkably intolerant of 'certain' differences, especially those pertaining to human sexuality.

The strength of this book lies in the ways in which the various authors and their respective chapters are, in their own way, wrestling with these enduring dialectics as they pertain to Baptist identity. We have essays that are wrestling with gender and patriarchy, reflecting on the challenges for women undertaking ministry in context. Ditto, there are chapters that address Black cultural identity and Black heritage, detailing how the Baptist tradition can be a conduit for the flourishing of Blackness in its many guises and perspectives, although not without its

229

considerable challenges. The issue of sexuality is addressed as is nationality and language, the latter operating outside of the normative posture of Englishness, often seen as a synonym for Britishness.

What is most admirable about this book, however, lies in the rootedness of the various contributions. The authors have largely eschewed the tendency in much academic theology to theologise in abstraction, ignoring the necessity of context and lived experience. As a Black theologian whose work lies at the intersectionality of liberation theologies and Practical theology, I have long believed that context and lived experience are essential dimensions of how we should think about Christian theology and its operation and relationship to the church. The essential identity of the Baptist tradition lies in the immediacy of the collective expression of being church together as the 'priesthood of all believers.'

Each of the eight chapters that comprise this book sheds light on the nature of ministry in context that exudes a reality and critical imagination for how the tradition can be renewed and developed. Working in a college in which a good deal of the Baptist tradition has been exemplified, perhaps, most tellingly in the towering figure of Professor Paul Fiddes, this book represents an alternative vista regarding Baptist identity in the UK. *Voicing New Questions for Baptist Identity* offers a number of important new insights and voices. In the emergence of younger women, Black voices, disabled voices, and the perspective of those who have suffered brokenness and disappointment, there is a realness and searing honesty that is potentially exciting, creative and challenging.

At a time when many ecclesial bodies are wrestling with issues of identity, their future, and how their respective churches can be renewed, in *Voicing New Questions for Baptist Identity*, we have an important new text that provides insights and creative engagement with issues of context, history and lived experience that speaks to the renewal of a tradition in the UK. I believe there is much that other traditions can learn from this book. This text is an important first!

Printed in Great Britain
by Amazon